Sharon Flynn

Ferment for good

Hardie Grant

BOOKS

Fermented food may be the slowest and oldest fast food. The main ingredients in fermenting are your desire to play and time to wait. Some curiosity, a bit of optimism and an ability to embrace naivety helps too. There's no need to think too hard because fermenting is the oldest way of planning for future needs. The skills are in our DNA. Alone in a kitchen or by coming together with others to make large batches, you can preserve a season. Time may have become a scarce commodity, but using your time to ferment so you can eat later, maybe even on the run, or in a hurry, is an investment you'll not regret.

Avid
fermentations
(how my tumbleweed life snowballed into a business)

I am a person who kept fermenting stuff to the point that it turned into a business. Admittedly, I was both high with excitement and troubled about writing this book. How could I juggle this project alongside my small and growing business, my recently blended family of five kids and the partner that I want more time with? Simple: I am honoured to share my love and passion for fermentation, my recipes and stories, and a book will reach further than any workshop.

Through my many moves, I have always been drawn to fermentation. I spent a decade in Japan, where a local grandma, a chef down the road and the local volunteer fire brigade became like family, and I learnt about miso, nattō and sake lees. In Chicago it was pickles, mustards and horseradish. Then in Seattle we were part of an amazing CSA (Community Supported Agriculture) scheme that held workshops on preserving extras. I also found milk kefir – it reminded me of the buttermilk I had enjoyed in Denmark as a student. I can thank all of the places I have lived for all of the foods I love and learnt to ferment.

Before all that, I'd spent a couple of years in Kuala Lumpur, Malaysia, for my dad's work. The smells and tastes of the street food and the food cooked by our *amah* will stay with me forever. Not long after we returned to Australia, I went to Denmark for a year as an exchange student. I lived on an old pig farm and ate open sandwiches, lots of fish and hung out in the kitchen cellar learning from my Danish host mum. A few years after coming back home, I went to Japan and really didn't return to Australia properly for 20 years, with three kids in tow.

Just before I returned, we were living in Brussels and I was desperately working on healing a little gut. My five-year-old had become very sick over a prolonged period and had been given so many different antibiotics that her gut must have been devoid of any life at all. Her development was regressing and, unable to keep any food down, she seemed to be fading away. She hadn't been to school in months and would walk stiff-legged on her toes and hardly speak to anyone. She couldn't walk more than a couple of metres without tiring or vomiting.

A friend told me that fermented foods such as yoghurt, milk kefir and sauerkraut might help. But I knew there were more living foods than just those, and if this were to work then a diverse array of living bacteria would need to get into her body and stay and grow there – and achieving this at each meal became my focus.

This was where I was suddenly able to draw a connection between my various food passions. I had been flirting with this kind of food preservation since my early 20s, but it wasn't until then that it occurred to me that, while my many fads seemed so different, they all came under the banner of fermentation. Mozzarella, sourdough, nattō, miso, pickles – every move had had its new books and manic trialling period. I had bought Sandor Katz's book *Wild Fermentation* very early on and loved it. But a sick little gut brought it all together for me.

I loved seasonal food but I didn't care about preservation; I cared only about providing diverse ferments and gorgeous flavours that my family would crave. Diversity and flavour are still important to me because my ferments need to be enjoyed and eaten regularly if they are to be medicinal in any way. I've no interest in hiding ferments in other food, nor do I want them to be thought of as purely medicinal – something you 'take'.

I madly started fermenting everything and passionately soapboxed about beneficial bacteria and the importance of gut health to any mildly curious new friends who'd see my kitchen full of crocks and carboys and, with lifted eyebrows, ask what the hell I was doing.

Initially, it was my water kefir that people loved. A few friends and mums from the school bus stop loved it and consequently craved it so much they wanted to buy a bottle (or six). I offered to teach them to make their own, but they just wanted to buy some – regularly and reliably. In the early, panic-stricken days of solo parenting, this was a small glimpse of an idea – an awakening for me.

POUNDING CABBAGE

Word got around at school that I was selling a 'healthy, probiotic-rich fizzy drink', and soon I was making dozens to sell out of my car boot (trunk). I felt rather rogue and like the chick from *Weeds*. Some late nights, when I was trying to work out if a keg would be good, or how to make a new ferment altogether, I imagined I was like the dude from *Breaking Bad*.

Eventually, I would just leave my car boot unlocked in the school car park so people could open it up, take what they'd ordered from the esky (cooler) and leave their money in an empty bottle. (It can be quite hard to get plastic Australian notes out of a bottle sometimes – more reminiscent of a desperate kid raiding a moneybox than the sexy chick from *Weeds*.)

Soon enough, through word of mouth, I had strangers calling to tell me all about their own ailments, or a friend or family member's health issues. Those phone calls were usually long because people are always relieved to be heard. Mostly, it was about bowel movements, allergies, skin disorders, autism spectrum, anxiety and depression, cancer or a suspected parasite. In return I gave them my own experience, my ear and my ferments.

I would drive an hour to drop off bottles to strangers. Sometimes I would go in and talk (for what I'm sure felt like hours for my kids waiting in the car). Other people even left their keys in a spot for me so I could deliver straight to their fridges, the money in an envelope on the bench. A couple of them came and worked for me here and there, and became key to getting my ferments into their favourite shops later on.

Some of them became friends, and all of that driving around made for a quick education in a new city. I was all over Melbourne in a huge car built for the country roads around Daylesford (a lovely country town an hour and a half north-west of Melbourne), not city traffic lights.

I'd show the kids my small wad of money on the way home and exclaim, 'An idea into reality – a tangible thing from thoughts in my head!' They were just as impressed as me.

As soon as the water kefir and krauts went into the local health food shop, the owner from another shop in a nearby town saw them and called. I agreed to drive the two hours there and back to deliver some. I hung up and wondered when I'd be able to do that; the town was in the opposite direction to Melbourne. I also knew that I wasn't making a profit despite all the activity. Soon afterwards, I got a call from a Sydney restaurant. Again, not really a profitable venture, but I was excited by it and I made the second delivery to Sydney myself. (That's a long road trip!)

The ball was rolling and I wasn't even pushing it. In fact I needed it to stop because I had no idea how to upscale. Nevertheless I added fridges and tanks and kept going. I learnt as I went; gained new partners and soon lost them as they realised it wasn't very profitable, no longer a hobby, or was different to what they'd imagined.

I look back in awe of that period of simultaneously working part time at a school, solo-parenting my kids, making and bottling up my ferments at night and delivering them on weekends between drop-offs to choir and music. But I'd started a small fire – I'd wake up with burning excitement, movement in my heart and a head full of thoughts, plans and dreams. It was also exhausting and a time of uncertainty, but I had created something and I loved every second of it. I also felt I was doing important and serious work – there were so many people just starting to learn about gut health and bacterial imbalance and I truly wanted to help them.

I met Roger – a veteran Melbourne chef – when I hired him to help me organise my 'procedures'. We both got more than we were expecting and

I soon had a new dedicated business partner and later, a new love that had time to grow as we spent many hours in the kitchen together.

We continue to grow our artisan micro-business. Staying true to techniques and beliefs and not changing them to upscale is a challenge. We're lucky we still have naivety, curiosity and optimism keeping us afloat, and our early customers to lean on for support and advice. The Daylesford people became my mentors and a source of confidence for me. I am eternally grateful to them, as well as to my first loyal Melbourne and Sydney customers.

In November 2015, I took a quick trip to Tennessee for a residency with Sandor Katz – author, father of the fermentation revival and enigmatic human in the world. For the first time in years I was hanging with people in my niche, learning from a master and camping out in a tent alone. Dizzy and exulted from my stay, I popped into Detroit to check out The Brinery, which happened to be near old friends from my days in Belgium.

We caught up with our lives, and they listened to my excited rant on fermenting, and all about my new business. I promised to send them recipes. Back in Melbourne, I went through old emails to find recipes, adjusted them with extra information for my friends and added an accompanying passionate spiel, because like any good zealot, I wanted my friends to catch my fervour and love it all as much as me.

And so! Welcome. You are now part of that group and pretty much holding those same recipes, my thoughts and rants about the ferments, why I love them, how to eat them, some ideas on how to expand on my recipes yourself and – most importantly – how to share this knowledge.

The sharing is very important because these are techniques that have survived and been cherished through time – handed down for generations. Kefir and yoghurt cultures alone have beginnings traceable only in folklore. Yet here we are, thousands of years on, holding them because they were not only a necessity for preserving food, but a tradition, a delight: taught, shared and treasured.

From the very first jar of kraut I hung a personally designed label on, I wanted the person buying it to feel like they were receiving it from an old friend – one who desperately wanted to share her discovery and passion with them. My goal hasn't changed at all: it is the same with this book, and for you. It can be rather contagious. I hope you'll join me. x

What is fermenting?

People all over the world, all the way back, have developed many different ways of reliably preserving their harvest for later. We've done this by drying, pickling, salt curing, locking out air with specific vats, crocks and oils, or by wrapping and burying meat, fish or vegetables in the ground. We've frozen, heated, brined and fermented.

Some of these methods rely on killing the life that would otherwise rot and decay the food. Probably the most common way of achieving sterility is by heating the food in its jar – known as pickling or canning, or simply preserving. This is an effective way of enabling produce to sit at room temperature, shelf-stable, for many years.

Fermented food, on the other hand, relies on its environment and the life on and in raw foods to preserve it. The bonus is that new textures, aromas and deeper flavours develop. And if that's not enough, fermented foods are full of living bacteria, yeasts and enzymes that enhance the food nutritionally and make other foods more digestible.

In fermentation, any pathogenic bacteria die a natural death due to the changes in the environment they are in. This leaves the remaining population – those who thrive in that specific environment, with those ingredients – to go ahead and preserve the food, usually by consuming the available natural sugars and converting them into a range of acetic or lactic acids, alcohol and carbon dioxides, etc. For instance, the sour flavours found in kefir, yoghurt, kraut and kimchi are the work of lactic acid bacteria, and with vinegar and kombucha, it's acetic acid bacteria.

There are foods you probably know are fermented – kombucha, sauerkraut, yoghurt, wine and beer – but chocolate, mead, coffee, cheese, cultured butter, sourdough breads, soy sauce, gherkins, cured meats and fish are fermented as well. The other lesser-known ferments include kimchi, dhosa, idli, injera, milk kefir, water kefir, and varieties of ferments made with the Japanese fungi kōji and nattō. The list is endless because how you adapt and harness this process is up to your imagination. Once you've prepared the food and waited for it to ferment, it's generally ready to eat with hardly any other preparation. Grab and go – nature's slowest fast food!

FERMENTED HONEY & GARLIC [PAGE 200]

Why I love fermentation

I love imagining the serendipitous way in which fermented foods must have been first discovered. There must certainly have been bravery and patience at play while figuring out the difference between rotten and controlled fermentation – and an acceptance to let accidents turn into new worlds of food.

Importantly for me, fermenting provides a sense of time and place, a call to milk the seasons. And while it requires routine and care that can feel as demanding as a child at times, the rhythm and continuity is quite comforting.

It was probably the wonder of the microscopic unknown, quite invisible, that I loved first though. Bringing that alchemy to my everyday routine opened my mind to so many other possibilities. It brought science, art and life into my kitchen. It's a tangible reminder that I don't control everything (it is not an exact science) and there is unseen magic in the everyday. This kind of earthy food preparation also provides a sense of connection to ancestors and to other traditions around the world.

I have always been the type of person who finds pleasure and comfort in the kitchen, but fermenting has brought that to another level altogether, and in a life-changing way. Long-term projects are very healthy; and when you move a lot your ferments can usually come with you in some form, unlike a garden.

People have been carrying their ferments with them for centuries. In fact, the recipes, kitchen cultures, fungi and SCOBYs that exist now do so purely because people all over the world and throughout time have nurtured and saved them. They have been passed down over many lifetimes, through drought, famine, war and migration, and changed environments and ideals. Or, more happily, exchanged and gifted through marriage, extended families and exciting journeys but, usually, I imagine, in the most basic of conditions. Heirloom cultures still exist whose journey you are welcome to be part of – or indeed, will become a part of you, a part of your life, to add to, share and hand down.

The art is in creating delicious ferments, and the science is obviously in organising the environment – the vessel, temperature, ingredients and pH – to a perfect point. The work is in learning to trust the process, your own intuition and, most importantly, your senses. Work on patience. Slow down and know that your gut bacteria will guide your palate to crave sour and complex over simple and sweet – if you let it. Forgive yourself your failures and share your favourites. Nurture your skill and show it to others.

Over the years, companies have found ways to process foods that were originally fermented into imitations of the real thing that sometimes even skip the fermentation part altogether. The reinvigoration of home fermenting has come about because we are discovering how far commercially produced foods have strayed from the real thing. Once you know how, the reward of making your own is immeasurable.

Ferment your own food because you can't buy a lot of the foods in this book as easily as you can other produced foods. Raw, wild-fermented foods aren't easily exported and they are hard to make commercially. You can get them from a good local artisan fermenter and at independent grocers or whole-food specialty shops. Or you can make them yourself at home.

Therefore, the aim of my book is to give you the confidence (and hopefully passion) to learn which fermented foods and drinks your palate, gut and curiosity crave most, and how to get your own little living, bench-top farm from your kitchen into the bodies of the people you love. Or just your own.

Wild fermentation

For me, fermenting is magical and satisfying when the process is as 'from scratch' as possible – spontaneous, wild and witchy. Wild fermentation is the ancient way of providing the right environment and the right ingredients and letting time take over.

Wild fermentation is where you create that alchemy without using any special tablets of yeast or packets of starter cultures – nothing made in a laboratory. Where would the mystery be in that? (See page 33 for more on why I don't use starter cultures.) There are many people who prefer to use powders, aiming for a higher probiotic content, or a guaranteed successful ferment, which makes me sad. Go ahead and do this if you like, but there aren't any recipes in this book that use starter cultures from a packet.

Wild fermentation is not only about the flavours and textures (which can change slightly per batch), but the history and connection to our ancestors, the wait, the connection to our food system, and the seasons you can save for later. That connection to the past is why none of the recipes in this book require luxury foods, nor do I insist you need expensive equipment. This technique of preservation has been around since well before fancy equipment came into existence, so keep that in mind.

IN YOUR DESIRE FOR SUCCESSFUL & ENJOYABLE FERMENTS IT'S BEST TO HAVE:

TIME & CONNECTION

At the top of my love list about fermenting is the time aspect. This is where you can lose yourself in the present every day because fermented food and drinks often become long-term projects.

The act of slowing down and anticipating the outcome for weeks, quite often months, and sometimes even years, is inextricably both calming and exciting. Like planting a seed, it brings hope for the future.

WHAT YOU'LL GET IN RETURN:

LIFE & THE ACCOMPANYING SOUNDS

I love the sounds of home: music – even repetitive and basic piano practice; people talking at the kitchen table; the clanking of a spoon in a tea cup; our front gate creaking, followed by the front door slamming when family arrive home. Fermenting has its own set of accompanying sounds. The gurgle of a crock bubbling is a soothing, nurturing and exciting sound. Often a few days after you've whipped up your batch of whatever, it'll start making beautiful bubbling noises in your kitchen. The bubbles confirm that you did a good job. It's a predictable and welcome sound because you know for sure that the alchemy has begun. You gathered all of the ingredients, made sure of the right environment and in return it has started working, happily doing the rest of the job for you. If you are using a ceramic crock, the sounds are really all you'll get until you open it up.

The bubbling noise always makes me smile. The last person up, late at night, showered, slip and slippers on and ready for bed, I'm emptying the dishwasher. 'Hello,' it says. 'I'm still working too.' I go over to the crock and tinker. I fill the water trap up a bit, wanting desperately to open it up and taste it to see if it's sour and crunchy, or (quite unlikely, but you never know) ruined and mushy. I check the water level in the moat on the huge crock. I peek into my soy sauce, god it smells good; I dip in a finger and taste. Crazy! Can't wait to see how it tastes in a year; I hope it will come into its own and ferment the way I've planned. In those moments, time has slipped and I've gone into a different, long-term mode. I look at the dates I've taped to the sides of jars and vats. I count how long it's been, and how long it'll be until I can drink it or eat it or jar or bottle it up and pop it into the fridge. I'm planning to give jars to friends this weekend, which might be too soon for this batch. I eagerly pop it in a warmer spot, which might speed it up a bit. I start imagining how much they'll like this batch; what they'll eat with it; and if they'll feel anything good happen in their guts and crave more. I look at my bottles of mead too and start thinking about the day that I'll bring them out, on my daughter's 18th birthday, two years away. Hopefully it'll taste good to her. I give the bottles a turn, or a pat and some love because two years is far away and I don't really want to imagine her being that old. Back to emptying the dishwasher.

YOU'LL ALSO GET:

GREAT-TASTING, FAT-CUTTING FOOD … & SOME UMAMI, PERHAPS

Ancient techniques, connection and gut health would mean much less if your ferments didn't taste good in the end, right? The flavours produced by natural fermentation are endless and unique. What is sweet becomes tart, what is flat, fizzy. Milk becomes sour, creamier and sometimes effervescent; beans become sticky and cheesy; grains sour and the textures change. Umami is becoming an overused term perhaps, but fermentation is the key to *real* umami, or the Japanese 'fifth taste' (see page 165 for more on umami).

MOST IMPORTANTLY, HEALTHY, GUT-HEALING FOOD

When your gut bacteria are balanced and strong, it's more likely that the rest of your body and mind will be too. The bacteria fermenting in your jars are going to grow and one day live inside the people who eat them. And we are seeking a large and diverse variety of bacteria inside us to give gut democracy a chance. Imbalance can happen for so many reasons, and can be exacerbated by the antibiotics in medicine or in our water and food, as well as chlorine and chemical residue in our water and the overuse of antibacterial products. This war against bacteria happened not too long ago and we innocently, fervently, joined in with wipes, sprays and gels in our homes, cars and handbags.

There aren't actually good and bad bacteria in a healthy body. We need them all. It's when there is an imbalance that one becomes bad and we call on others to balance things out. All the bacteria on and in our bodies can balance out as long as we aren't constantly doing things to kill them off.

When you kill 'bad' bacteria – the germy ones that might make you ill, or cause bad breath, for example – you are also killing the 'good' bacteria. Wiping out all of them means the survivors have to build their own community from what's left. If you make sure to eat a variety

of fermented foods frequently, you'll be giving your gut every chance to build a balanced world. Eating fermented foods should be a constant way of eating – not something you 'take' and then put away for when you are sick again.

Research into our microbiome and the connection between gut health and our general health is advancing so fast – it's fascinating and important. This is a recipe book, so I'm going to leave the advanced gut health part to your own investigations and other more qualified people. But I do know that over the years I have watched a lot of people heal guts, anxiety, depression, inflammation and constipation by incorporating these foods into their diets – often enough to know I'm speaking the truth.

Unfortunately, our palates have changed to prefer the flavour of processed foods – lots of kids, for instance, prefer the sweet and only mildly tangy shop-bought yoghurt to the homemade kind. But given the encouragement, and the story and the knowledge of what they're eating – the love involved in preparing it – they turn around to loving the real thing pretty quickly.

Here's a bonus: eating ferments can help balance taste buds and gut bacteria, thereby influencing diet choices. Eventually you will crave sour and fresh over sickly sweet or bland. I noticed this straight away in my daughter Lulu as her gut healed. She went from craving simple carbohydrates like pasta and bread to wanting kefir and krauts and, in particular, kimchi juice. It seemed like a crazy miracle back then. Her moods and her health improved simultaneously with her palate. I think anyone who's started exercising after a long break would know that feeling. When your body starts feeling good you start craving more movement and better foods. Children are no different. Given the chance and, importantly, the support, they choose real foods.

YOU CAN ALSO ENJOY: LIFE, A GARDEN

If you have a few things going and bubbling on your bench or in your pantry – and you tinker with them, look after them, check on them – you have a kind of garden. If, like me, you don't have a green thumb, or space to have a soil garden, this is your answer. You provide an environment that controls the opportunity for growth within a preservation context. This quite calming, simple practice includes a small amount of pottering, dreaming and tinkering.

The microscopic creatures involved in fermenting form the easiest kind of garden there is, and the process is tremendously rewarding – no digging or building of waist-high garden beds, nor any weeding or netting. This garden produces sounds, smells, delicious fare and provides a healthy return on your efforts. It requires the humblest equipment, and if you allow the right environment for growth, closing a lid on a ferment is not that different from pushing soil over a seed. All you need to do is wait patiently for the invisible magic that is nature – right there in your kitchen.

Some terms & words

BACK-SLOPPING: the practice of using a little bit of a finished product to start up a new batch, for instance using yoghurt as a starter of another batch. It's used in fermenting a lot.

BONITO FLAKES (KATSUOBUSHI): dried, smoked and fermented bonito or skipjack tuna shavings.

CROCK: an earthenware pot or jar. In fermentation it usually refers to one that comes with a lid surrounded by a small moat to hold water and act as an air-lock. Often comes with weights that fit the crock just right.

DAIKON: Japanese or white radish. It literally means 'big root' but is known by other names, depending on where you are. They are the thick, long, white ones with large leaves. Best in mid-winter.

DULSE FLAKES: a red sea lettuce/algae. Like all seaweeds, we've been eating them or feeding them to animals forever. They are full to the brim with goodness – minerals, vitamins, trace elements, and are high in protein too! All seaweeds make for excellent healthy snacks or sprinkles. Comes in various forms, but the flakes are great on eggs and through krauts.

KOMBU: an edible seaweed that is frequently used in Japanese cooking, often as a stock base.

LEES/KASU: the remainder of something – for example, the remaining yeast and pressed grapes after winemaking, or the pressed rice after sake making. Sake lees can be bought in sheet form or in soft form depending on how it is pressed.

MOTHER: a mother is a community of micro-organisms that start a ferment. For example, a kombucha SCOBY is called a mother.

NATTŌ: Japanese soy beans fermented with *Bacillus subtilis* (var. nattō). This stringy bean ferment is found in various forms around the world and was historically made from grasses and leaves. This kind of bacteria is very strong and hard to kill. This makes it perfect health food as it gets into a gut and survives all the way down. Nattō can be an acquired taste but it's full of vitamin K2 and also has nattokinase, which is a beneficial protein enzyme preventing blood clots (so is well worth getting used to!).

SCOBY: stands for 'symbiotic colony of bacteria and yeast'. These occur in nature and under the right conditions will grow and reproduce while fermenting your drink for you. These include the little polysaccharide matrix kefir, milk kefir, kombucha, jun tea cultures and vinegar mothers.

TEFF: these grains are tiny and are more a grass than a grain. They are very nutritious and stem from Ethiopia where, because of their size, they have not traditionally been traded widely, but kept in the hands of the people who grow it. This is a gluten-free grain and the star ingredient for the lovely injera (page 211) – an enormous pancake-like bread.

WAKAME: another sea vegetable – you buy this dried in sheets or crumbled. Used mostly in dashi (stock) and miso soups. Has been eaten in Japan for hundreds of years.

WOMBOK: also known as Napa cabbage or Chinese cabbage, it's a sweet, long, curly and softer kind of cabbage.

Some stuff to know first

(or read later)

Vegetables can be fermented in the most basic conditions – even spontaneously or by accident. But as I was writing the first very simple kraut recipe (page 36), so many small but important details came to mind and unless you grew up with a fermenter in your house, some of these do merit at least a bit of discussion. If details aren't your thing, just follow the recipes and refer back to the information given here as your questions arise.

Remember though: the idea that a vegetable can contain the power or life to ferment itself spontaneously is fascinating. The process is so simple and the ingredients can be even simpler. The equipment is humble and can usually be found in your kitchen (or shed). The process can be as basic as cutting the vegetable, adding the right amount of salt, packing it in the right vessel correctly, considering where to put it and how long to wait.

WHAT TEMPERATURE TO FERMENT AT: 12–21°C (54–70°F) – BASICALLY ROOM TEMPERATURE

Temperatures required for lactic acid fermentation are easily achievable, but consistency is quite important – an average kitchen is usually warmer in the day and much cooler in the middle of the night, so try to place your ferments in a spot that has the least variation. Using a heat pad or electric blanket or wrapping the vessel in a towel helps in a cold environment.

In my opinion, the best vegetable ferments result from lower temperatures because the fermentation is slow enough to allow for complex flavours to develop – aim for around 12–21°C (54–70°F). Try to keep the temperature no higher than 21°C (70°F), as temperatures warmer than this will speed up the process and increase the risk of spoilage. Environs too cool will slow down and even stunt your ferment.

HOW LONG TO FERMENT FOR: IT'S READY WHEN IT'S DELICIOUS

To make this decision, use your most ancient monitor: your senses. Waiting for something makes it more exciting! This is also true for slow food. How long you'll have to wait depends on all of the variables: the ingredients, and their accompanying 'terroir' – the salt quantity, quality and variety; the temperature; the type of vessel; how you've packed that vessel; and your method of keeping it anaerobic (meaning an absence of air).

Depending on all of the above variables, the first stages of fermentation are completed anywhere between three and six days – particularly with ferments of softer vegetables; lots of different vegetables; or ones that already have a ferment in them to kickstart them, as kimchi does if you add a good soy or fish sauce. (Kimchi tends to be a fast ferment and can be enjoyed from the moment you make it.)

Sauerkraut and many brined vegetables take a bit longer. The lactic acids increase and change and you'll decide if they are ready by tasting them. I recommend two weeks minimum, but personally aim for six weeks.

Smaller amounts tend to ferment faster, and therefore larger batches often taste better because complex flavours really develop over time.

WHAT KIND OF VESSEL TO USE: SOMETHING OLD, SOMETHING NEW, FROM THE KITCHEN OR SHED

There are a plethora of lovely vessels you can buy or put on a wish list to use in fermenting. It is one of the lovely things about a hobby or a period of *zanmai* (a Japanese word meaning 'to be luxuriously absorbed in something'; see page 213). And foraging is not just for blackberries or wild mustard seeds, but also for cool-looking jars, bottles, vessels, crocks, weights, fabric and muslin (cheesecloth). You can use any vessel you have in your house – you don't even need a lid really. I've made a lot of kimchis, krauts and brines in glass jars on my kitchen bench without worrying about light and they've been fine.

Enjoy searching for the many options of gorgeous porcelain or clay crocks, special fermenting jar systems, swing-top bottles and air-lock systems, but take into consideration the following:

— I like glass jars for small amounts – especially if you want to do a few different ferments at a time. There are a variety of well-designed, high-quality air-locking lidding systems available. You can also use food-grade plastic containers – there

are some fabulous Korean and Japanese food-grade plastic pickle presses available that are made with food-grade plastic. A lot of the faster Japanese pickles are even commonly fermented in zip-lock bags. Not very traditional, but they do the job.

— Darkness is preferable to light, so clay crocks are my favourite. Crocks automatically provide darkness, but if using a glass jar and there's direct light, you can easily pop a cloth over it or keep it in a dark cupboard. Don't let your ferment sit in the sun, because that kind of light and heat is too intense.

— A crock is also better at maintaining temperature, but make sure it has been made with lead-free glaze. Many crocks tend to be quite big and, although you'll be surprised at how much you'll consume, in the beginning they are probably too big for the average home. You could perhaps use a larger crock as a way to get friends and family over to do a 'kraut mob' and then jar it and share it out once it's ready (see page 42).

(see page 42).

— With a large crock, be aware that the weight of the vegetables and brine you're putting in significantly adds to its weight. I have made a batch in my big crock only to find that I have had to leave it right there on the bench because it was just too heavy to move.

— I have a beautiful porcelain crock that was made for me by a friend whom I adore, and everyone who comes to our kitchen admires it. But I've also had a German crock from the beginning of my fermenting journey and an old Korean one because that's just what I had. I usually use the large crock for a plain kraut and smaller jars for other vegetables and 'experi-ferments'.

Once you are obsessed and enjoying your ferment *zanmai*, go ahead and shop around for the equipment that you covet.

STERILISATION & CLEANLINESS

A very clean environment is essential, but you don't need to use any strong antibacterial washes that promise to kill surface bacteria. We are trying to harness life, remember! A hot dishwasher will do, or sterilise your equipment with boiling water swished in and around and leave to air-dry. We often use citric acid and boiling water, so if you need to use something stronger, that's what I recommend.

If a completely sterile environment is needed, as I instruct for some ferments (for sauces that you'd like to be shelf stable, for example), after an initial wash you can place your vessel onto a tray in a hot oven at 180°C (350°F) and leave to dry in the oven for approximately ten minutes. Do not put the jar on the floor of the oven as contact with direct heat can cause breakage – if not immediately, later on, because the glass has been weakened.

AIR-LOCK SYSTEM: LET IT OUT & KEEP IT OUT

Lactobacillus thrives in anaerobic environments. However, carbon dioxide, which is the result of a happy ferment, needs a way to escape. It's the by-product of the yeasts and bacteria feeding on the sugars. If too much pressure builds, there may be breaks, spills or seeps.

You get a better, more predictable and delicious ferment by using an air-lock system. It's the easiest method, as you don't have to think about letting the gas out manually, and it creates a healthier environment for the ferment. It's effective because you can leave an air-locked jar alone for the whole fermenting time, and if the brine isn't that plentiful, then you are still providing an anaerobic environment for the bacteria.

Homemade air-lock systems are simple and cheap to put together. You can buy an S-bend air-lock at home brewery shops (or online, of course) and fit it into a drilled hole in a normal jar lid. Make sure your air-lock comes with a little rubber stopper to line the hole. Fit your air-lock, fill it halfway with water, and put the lid on. Purpose-made jars that come with the air-lock system fitted abound and are easily found in shops and online. I have many of these systems that I love.

In the absence of an air-lock system, you can wrap plastic wrap around the lid as it stretches. Even more fun is a balloon on a bottle, or a thin rubber glove on a jar (see page 77 for a photo of this). As the gases form they fill up! SO fun.

If you have a water trap or moat system, as with a crock, you simply fill the moat up as much as possible, and leave it. As gases form they escape through the lid, but the water stops any air from getting in. The downside is that the water evaporates. You need to make sure you fill up the moat regularly because if the water evaporates all the way, and your moat is dry, air will get in and may ruin the top of your ferment, at the very least.

The simplest and cheapest way of all is to rely on the brine to cover your ferment. If you choose to use a jar without a lid, you need enough brine to cover your ferment completely – first by using a cover like a cabbage leaf or a suitably sized plate, then a weight and a secured cloth or towel over the top to keep bugs away. I've personally never liked this system but lots of people, including Sandor Katz, use it, as do a lot of larger fermenting businesses. The reason I don't like it is that I don't always have enough brine for this – I don't ever want to add water to a ferment (it would water the flavour down) and I don't like having to check on it constantly to make sure the ferment is still covered.

SALTING EN
MASSE!

Another very reasonable option is simply a jar with a lid. You just need to leave enough head room and burp it every day or from time to time. A jar with a flip-top lid and rubber ring is also great as it both releases some gases itself and is easier to open and close quickly.

On the other side of the coin are the ferments that are aerobic. This means that they WANT exposure to the air and just need to be covered with cloth or paper towel for cleanliness and to keep the bugs away. This is particularly important with kombucha and vinegar – bugs love that stuff.

SALT: FINE, PURE & WELL DISTRIBUTED

Unless I am packing a jar with salt for a dry salt ferment, in which case I use a coarser salt, I prefer finely ground salt. Make sure to always distribute your salt well and evenly. With kraut, the salt draws water from the cabbage cells and this water becomes your brine and supports the development of anaerobic conditions that you need for lactic acid fermentation. It also slows fermentation down, giving it time to reach the right pH.

I recommend a finely ground Celtic sea salt – but any will do, just make sure it's natural with no iodine or additives. It's even better if you can use something local; you may be surprised how many local salts there are when you look. Salt is a very interesting ingredient to know more about – so many different kinds and flavours.

The aim is to keep the good salt-loving bacteria alive and strong while the bad soggy-cabbage-causing-bacteria die off. Over time, especially in the first few days, the flora will change – one kind will have power then die, while the next take over, until the acid-loving lactic acid bacteria take over for good. Your salt ratio will depend on the salinity of the salt and the type of vegetable you're fermenting with, so you may need to fiddle with amounts if you are using a special kind of salt.

Indeed, the amount of salt you add affects everything – from the speed of your ferment to the microbial population and of course the flavours. Too little and you'll get a soft ferment and the wrong kind of microbial diversity – more of a decomposing situation rather than fermentation. I think anywhere from 1.5–3% is fine. Aim for 2% and be as precise with this as you can. Also, keep in mind that when it is warmer, you may add a bit more salt, and when it is cooler, a bit less. As vegetables vary in weight and size, I recommend you weigh them after shredding and chopping, and then work out your salt ratio from there.

FRESH IS BEST – ROTTING CAN RUIN YOUR FERMENT

When you are choosing vegetables to ferment, apply the same principles you would if you were making a salad and about to eat it raw – because you are. Fermenting, in particular for brines and krauts, isn't a great time to use the old damaged stuff. You can use older produce for vinegars and ciders, even for kefir and kombucha second ferments, but vegetable ferments work best with the freshest produce possible. It's also best to simply wash the vegetables really well rather than peel them. (I do tend, however, to peel tougher-skinned vegetables like daikon/white radish and certainly sweet potato.) Vegetables are coated in and are full of the very stuff we want to encourage, particularly if they've come from good, healthy soil, and a lot of the good yeasts and bacteria are found on the skin.

Obviously organic is best, but there's no need to be pedantic, or simply trust organic for the sake of it – be a smart organic buyer. There may be a lot of small farmers around you that don't have certification because they are too small, but who care for their land and soil and the food it produces. I choose fresh, local produce (and from small farms) over organic produce from far away, particularly when it comes to cabbage. Fermentation itself rids your food of any trace pesticides, and cabbage is one of the 'clean 15' vegetables – meaning that it is one of the lesser-sprayed vegetables. So it's fine to buy regular cabbage – you peel so many of the outer leaves off anyway.

ON POUNDING

'Next ... walk out to the shed and grab an axe handle.' That's a line from my great aunt's kraut recipe. For krauts and kimchis you need to

POUNDING HELPS THE VEGIES
RELEASE THEIR JUICES

ABOVE: AN ASSORTMENT OF TRADITIONAL WEIGHTS
RIGHT: AN ORGANIC WEIGHT

massage and mix the salt through evenly, and then pound the cabbage to coax out the water from within to make a natural brine. Instead of an axe handle, you can just find something from your kitchen to pound with – the end of a rolling pin, a large strong potato masher, or similar. There are some beautiful purpose-built pounders that are lovely to hold and simply to have in your kitchen, especially if you are going to do this a lot. Even easier, if you have a stand mixer with a dough hook on it, you can pop the salted vegies in there – this is a very quick method. Letting them sit in salt to draw the water out works too. You could even clean some feet and let them do the mashing – this is the old fashioned, romantic way, especially if you have a lot of cabbage to do. However, DON'T pound the cabbage IN your crock or jar! It's not designed for that – do the pounding in a bowl or large plastic tub first, before packing.

PACKING YOUR VESSEL

It's important to pack the vegetables tightly into the jar – the tighter the better, because this is the start of creating an anaerobic environment. Packing tightly also pushes the brine up to the surface, which is also your goal.

You can either use your pounder or your fist to firmly pack your kraut into your jar or crock.

You don't want too much room left at the top (as we are making an anaerobic environment, remember), but plan for a thumb length in a two litre (68 fl oz) jar, or a hand space in a huge crock. Don't forget you'll need to hold it all down under the brine with a follower and a weight, so leave room for those.

WEIGHTS & FOLLOWERS

A follower is a liner – simply something placed over the top of the vegetables before the weight, to help keep the vegetables down. The follower should be non-reactive and clean (a cabbage leaf, for example, or a plate even) and acts to stop little bits of the vegetable floating around and onto the weight.

In the first active stage of fermentation the gases will push through, moving your vegetables with them, so to keep them safely under the brine you can use anything heavy as long as it's very clean. There are many weights on the market now, but making do can be quite satisfying. Using a piece of vegetable such as a chunk of carrot, or a bit of red onion chopped

to the exact size you need works well – just ensure whatever you use is big enough so the lid pushes it down into the vegetables and holds them down. A vegetable can add a bit of flavour though, so choose with that in mind. A large rock is great; just boil it for about ten minutes to get rid of any unwanted dirt, and let it become your family heirloom fermenting rock.

Alternatively, you can use a water-filled plastic bag, or a muslin (cheesecloth) bag with pie weights in it; these can act as both a weight and an air lock. You can also use another jar – perhaps filled with water to make it heavier.

Sometimes it can be a challenge to find something that will fit into your jar, so you may need to get creative or go and buy some nice weights. (Crocks usually come with weights.) I also sometimes use a couple of Weck jar lids the size smaller than the jar.

Don't use plastics or metals that are reactive to acidic environments.

JARRING UP

If you are using a large crock you'll want to put your ferment into smaller jars to refrigerate when they are finished fermenting. Take out the weights, follower and perhaps even the top layer or first two and a half centimetres (one inch). With clean hands, put your ferment into clean jars, pack tightly, lid them, label them with the date and contents, and put into the fridge. With a smaller jar, just take out the weight and follower, change lids if needed and put it into the fridge as is.

USE YOUR SENSES

When you hear your first bubble, you know your ferment is active. This is why I like to use air-lock systems over jars or brine-covered vessels. I like to hear the action. Keep an eye on your work to make sure your water trap is full, or that your vegetables remain under the brine – if you aren't using a lidded system or crock you may need to push the weight down to keep it under the brine quite regularly.

Try to leave your ferment alone as much as you can. Use your senses to decide if it's ready: each ferment will let you know. If it's sour and fresh smelling then it's fine. It should look alive and shiny, smell sour, feel clean and taste fresh.

It shouldn't feel slimy, or smell too yeasty or sulphurous, nor should there be any colourful mould on the top.

Certainly, some vegetables make a pretty foul smell when fermented – like cauliflower; and yes okay, there's a point when sauerkraut makes a certain smell, and kimchi gives off a powerful odour – but none of the smells should be too nauseating or foul. And you'll know by the texture if it's good or not – we are preserving, not decomposing, remember. I've had batches that were a bit soft and then dug down a bit and found that they're fine underneath. While I'd obviously never do this for a commercial batch, digging down a few inches and finding the kraut shiny, living and fresh is a cool feeling.

We have had plenty of messy mistakes, many explosive results, batches that were fizzy, soggy or just plain un-tasty. Just like when you burn toast or ruin a salad dressing: scrape it off, toss it in the compost or be annoyed, but don't be discouraged. Cry if it's a huge batch and you needed a good cry anyway, or if you were catering for a party and trying to impress someone. Then go back and start again.

Once you feel your ferment is ready, put it in the fridge to slow the process right down, and to keep it at the same stage for a lot longer. It will still ferment and the flavours will change with time but at a much slower rate.

TO USE STARTER CULTURE OR NOT — UNLESS IT'S A SCOBY OR YOU'RE BACK-SLOPPING, WHY BOTHER?

As I've mentioned, I am not a fan of using a starter for vegetable ferments at all. People who come to me to buy starter cultures receive this lecture:

First, how do you think sauerkraut and kimchi and all the other ferments were made before packet starters? And why would bacteria grown in a laboratory on a substrate such as whey be safer than salt? Starter cultures are often sold as the safest, fastest guarantee of a good ferment but lactic acids are the best killers of other bacteria so there's no question of safety. When you use a starter culture you are no longer fermenting naturally, you're using a packet mix that usually contains only a few strains of bacteria. When you introduce these to the vegetables via the packet, the starter culture mimics what would happen during a natural ferment, essentially speeding up that process and limiting the amazing array of naturally occurring microbes already there. It feels like a 'just add water' project and indeed, you will need to add water to actually mix your starter through – which just adds to the watering down of the flavours – the *terroir* of your ferment will be lost. For me, the magic is gone. Be brave and harness the life that nature has provided. Adding a starter culture is not making something from scratch. It's a packet mix and not much different to using a powder to make custard or pancakes. Seriously.

HOW LONG DO THEY KEEP?

This is up to you – and depends on the temperature and vessel you've used. Our ferments take between two and six weeks in the vat and then we jar them and refrigerate. If they are stored properly in the fridge they are good for 12 months. It is even okay to freeze them in a bag if done correctly. You may need to keep an eye on the calendar if you have made a huge batch, but otherwise I'm sure you'll eat them all up way before 12 months comes around.

Vegetables

Krauts

Sauerkraut is an obvious best place to start; it's hard to ruin this, I promise.

Cabbage is perfect for fermenting because the cell walls are easily broken down with salt, and the juices that are released quite easily make the brine. While you are chopping and grating your cabbage, eat a piece raw. It will be crunchy and sweet. After fermentation it will be pretty crunchy still, shiny and alive-looking; the sugars will have been eaten by the lactobacillus bacteria (et al); and the *sauer* that you taste is the lactic acid cleverly produced by the lactobacillus. I'm salivating just writing this.

I prefer to use a large sharp knife for shredding, rather than a spindly little grater; the cut is better and the rhythm cathartic – keep the slices as even as possible. Having said that, food processors work well and slice evenly too; they are also easy to use and fast.

Or, try to get hold of a large wooden grater – they are beautiful. (I think we should all feel a bit ripped off for not getting one handed down from our parents. Remedy that by getting the right stuff and using it with a view to hand it on. Even your crocks and buckets can be heirlooms.)

Traditional sauerkraut (with caraway)

Preparation time: ↓1 hour
Fermentation time: 2–10 weeks
Equipment: 2 L (68 fl oz) jar, pounder, follower (cabbage leaf), weight

2 green cabbages (about 2 kg/4 lb 6 oz), shredded
50 g (1¾ oz) fine ground salt (about 2.5%)
15 g (½ oz) caraway seeds (optional)

Weigh the shredded cabbage (as cabbages vary in size and weight) to ensure the salt to cabbage ratio is correct. The amount of salt you use should come to about 1.5–2.5%, but no more than 3%, of the cabbage weight.

In a large bowl, mix and massage the salt through the cabbage thoroughly, making sure to distribute the salt evenly.

Let it sit to sweat a bit – maybe 10 minutes. This is simply to make the next step easier. This is a good time to get your vessel cleaned and to rest up for the next stage.

With your pounder, pound quite energetically for about 5–10 minutes, until the cabbage is dripping with its own salty water when you pick up a handful. This part is important as you need this liquid – it's your brine.

You can also use the dough hook of a stand mixer to do the pounding part, which can speed things up somewhat. Don't let it run for too long though, only a few minutes. Using a mixer is easy and great for people who are doing this a lot and in large batches, but it takes quite a bit of the emotional release and fun out of it. (See pages 28–30 for more on pounding.)

Next, mix in the caraway seeds (if using).

Put the mixture into the jar, packing it down tightly as you go using the pounder. Push down well, particularly at the end to coax out any more brine. You need the brine to cover the cabbage.

Don't pack the cabbage all the way to the top; leave some headroom at the top of the jar to allow for a bit of growth and movement and, of course, the weight. You don't want the liquid touching the top of the lid, as it will end up spewing out of your air-lock or up out of your lid.

Cover with a cabbage leaf (the follower), the weight and then your chosen lid or system. (See from page 26 for more on lidding systems, followers and weights.)

Depending on your ferment, you can start trying it as soon as you'd like, but the less you fiddle with it in the first 2 weeks, the better. It is ready when you think it is delicious. With the right system and temperature, you can leave it to ferment for months before refrigeration.

If you used a crock, you'll need to decant the kraut to smaller jars before you refrigerate, unless you have a walk-in cool room, or large cellar. (Lucky you.) It will keep in the fridge for 12 months or more. Use your senses.

OTHER KRAUT IDEAS TO PLAY WITH — SOME GOOD IDEAS FOR YOUR KRAUTING LIFE

I ferment firstly for flavour – there's no good telling my children that this or that is great for fighting colds ... they'll eat it medicinally, and under sufferance, but that is not the point. Make it delicious and the health benefits come naturally. We use different, almost obvious, combinations of vegetables in our krauts and there are definite benefits to each: immune boosting, liver cleansing, you name it. But most importantly, these combinations taste amazing. The end.

There are as many variations in sauerkraut as there are in soups, stir-fries, pasta sauces or sandwich toppings – you learn intrinsically what goes well together. Vegetables from the same family complement each other in a kraut. The suggestions that follow can be a guide until you start thinking up combinations, and salivating about them, yourself.

Use the regular techniques for making sauerkraut (see page 36), making sure to coax the juices from the cabbage using salt, patience and power, packing it in tightly, weighing and sealing properly. Keep in mind that if you add other vegetables, you should weigh them with the cabbage before you determine your salt ratio. Try to keep the cabbage to about 75% of the total weight. This rule helps keep your cabbage crunchy – too much sugar from the other vegetables and you could be in for some soggy ferments.

After you've mixed, massaged and pounded your salt and cabbage together thoroughly, add the other vegetables and any spices or seeds and mix them all in and through the cabbage until evenly dispersed. You can't over-mix this – the more the better really. Clean, bare hands love this, so pull your sleeves up and go for it – it's as joyous as putting your hands in soil.

Ideally, you'd shred a double amount of cabbage and make up the Traditional sauerkraut recipe (page 36) with one half and then use the rest of the cabbage to play with. At many of our workshops we plonk various grated vegetables and spices on the table and let people experiment with flavour by adding what they'd like to their batch. For those who are confident and love to play with flavours, here are some simple suggestions using the most common ingredients you can add to cabbage.

APPLE

A little goes a long way. Grate, slice or chop it. I often use whole, small apples as weights.

BEETROOT (BEET)

A little bit of beetroot grated or even sliced and added to your kraut is a gorgeous thing – to look at while it's fermenting, and then obviously to eat. It's sweet and earthy and bright pink. Watch out though – the sugar can ruin a batch. Stick to the 75% cabbage rule and you'll be fine.

CARROT

Grated or julienned carrot as an addition to your kraut gives it a sweetness and earthiness that's similar to beetroot.

CELERY SEED

This is a powerful little secret seed that goes well in any plain kraut. Is this the new caraway? Try making a red and green cabbage kraut with salt and celery seeds and see what happens.

CHILLI

Chilli is always a good idea. A dash of chilli with any kraut doesn't always make it into kimchi – in fact, there's a well-known kraut from South America called *cortido* that has oregano, chilli, carrot and sometimes a dash of pineapple brine or vinegar.

DILL

Fresh, flowers or seeds are all great for fermenting with.

FENNEL

Use the stalk or fronds, the seeds, or even the flowers. The aniseed flavour complements kraut well.

GARLIC

It's not just for kimchi – it can add depth to any kraut. Then add other ingredients that pair with garlic. Think parsley, lemon, garlic or capers. Or a little red chilli?

GINGER

Add it by the sliver, or tuck a large piece down the side, on the bottom or on the top, or grate finely and mix through. A little goes a long way, so be 'ginger' with it. Then think about what else might go with this magical warm root. Turmeric? Black pepper? Garlic?

HERBS, SPICES & OTHER BITS & PIECES

Try your favourite combinations of any of the following: star anise, cumin, cardamom, pepper, coriander seeds (or the root slid down the side), red onion, saffron threads, tarragon, shiso leaf, turmeric, juniper berry, oregano, curry leaf, bay leaf, caraway and mustard seeds.

LEEK

For a gentle onion flavour, add a leek to your kraut – wash well and slice as roughly as you'd like. Goes well with a bit of lemon and a sprinkle of chilli.

LEMON PEEL

Lemon peel zested or slivered into your kraut with garlic and dill is a pretty well-known combo and so fresh! It captures the flavour of summer and goes beautifully with Labneh (page 111).

If you need more specific instructions, here are a few tried and true recipes used by The Fermentary, a few of which have won awards. Treat the following recipes as ideas – if you don't have an apple, for example, swap it for a carrot or leave it out.

Carrot, turmeric & ginger kraut

Preparation time: 20–30 minutes
Fermentation time: 2–3 weeks
Equipment: 2 L (68 fl oz) jar, pounder, follower, weight

1 green cabbage, shredded
310 g (11 oz/2 cups) grated carrot
about 20–30 g (¾–1 oz) fine ground salt (check ratio)
2.5 cm (1 in) piece of fresh ginger, finely grated
5 cm (2 in) piece of fresh turmeric, grated
1 tablespoon ground black pepper
1 tablespoon cumin seeds

Weigh the cabbage and carrot and determine the salt measurement. Transfer the cabbage to a large bowl or container, sprinkle over the salt and let sit. Pound or massage to get all of the juices out – ideally enough so that if you pick up a handful of cabbage you'll have dripping water flowing from a clenched fist. Add the carrot and other ingredients and mix thoroughly. Pack tightly into your jar or crock, add the follower, and weigh down. Seal with your preferred system. Wait. Check for flavour after about 5 days. Refrigerate when ready – this usually takes 2–3 weeks.

It will keep in the fridge for up to 12 months.

Danish-inspired red kraut

Preparation time: 15–25 minutes
Fermentation time: 5+ days
Equipment: 2 L (68 fl oz) jar, pounder, follower, weight

2 red cabbages, shredded
about 50 g (1¾ oz) fine ground salt (check ratio)
10 g (½ oz) fennel seeds

Weigh the cabbage and determine the salt measurement. Transfer the cabbage to a large bowl or container, sprinkle over the salt and let sit. Pound or massage to get all of the juices out – ideally enough so that if you pick up a handful of cabbage you'll have dripping water flowing from a clenched fist. Add the apple and fennel seeds and mix thoroughly. Pack tightly into your jar or crock, add the follower, and weigh down. Seal with your preferred system. Wait. Check. If you use apple, it may be ready faster – check after 5 days.

It will keep in the fridge for up to 12 months.

Note: *This is great with salty meats like pork, on a cheese sandwich, over baked or creamy*
mashed potato (try it with crumbled feta), or in a salad.

Red fennel kraut

Preparation time: 30 minutes
Fermentation time: 2–3 weeks
Equipment: 2 L (68 fl oz) jar, pounder, follower, weight

2 red cabbages, shredded
1 kg (2 lb 3 oz) fennel bulbs, finely sliced (use less if you are after a milder fennel flavour)
2 apples, grated (optional)
about 75 g (2¾ oz) fine ground salt (check ratio)
1 teaspoon crushed juniper berries
¼ teaspoon celery seeds
1 teaspoon fennel seeds

Weigh the cabbage, fennel and apple (if using) and determine the salt measurement. Transfer the cabbage to a large bowl or container, sprinkle over the salt and let sit. Pound or massage to get all of the juices out – ideally enough so that if you pick up a handful of cabbage you'll have dripping water flowing from a clenched fist. Add the fennel and other ingredients and mix thoroughly. Pack tightly into your jar or crock, add the follower, and weigh down. Seal with your preferred system. Wait. It will probably take about 2–3 weeks to ferment.

It will keep in the fridge for up to 12 months.

Note: *This kraut goes well with pork sausages or chops, cheesy baked potatoes, blue cheese tart, quiche … get the picture?*

DISHED-UP DANISH-INSPIRED RED KRAUT

Beet red kraut

Preparation time: 20–30 minutes
Fermentation time: 2–3 weeks
Equipment: 2 L (68 fl oz) jar, pounder, follower, weight

2 red cabbages, shredded
140 g (5 oz/1 cup) grated beetroot (beet)
155 g (5½ oz/1 cup) grated carrot
1 apple, grated (optional)
about 30 g (1 oz) fine ground salt (check ratio – you're aiming for about 1.5% with this kraut)
10 g (¼ oz) coriander seeds
5 cm (2 inch) piece of fresh ginger, grated
5 g (¼ oz) cracked black pepper

Weigh the cabbage, beetroot, carrot and apple (if using) and determine the salt measurement. Transfer the cabbage and beetroot to a large bowl or container, mix, then sprinkle over the salt and let sit. Pound or massage to get all of the juices out – ideally enough so that if you pick up a handful you'll have dripping water flowing from a clenched fist. Add the carrot, apple and other ingredients and mix thoroughly. Pack tightly into your jar or crock, add the follower, and weigh down. Seal with your preferred system. Wait. Check. Refrigerate when ready – this usually takes between 2–3 weeks.

It will keep in the fridge for up to 12 months.

Smoky jalapeño kraut

This is The Fermentary's much-coveted recipe for our beloved kraut, which has quite a following in Melbourne.

Preparation time: 30 minutes
Fermentation time: 2–4 weeks
Equipment: 2 L (68 fl oz) jar, pounder, follower, weight

2 green cabbages, shredded
about 50 g (1¾ oz) fine ground salt (check ratio)
1 fresh jalapeño (if you like extra heat include the chilli membrane and seeds, if not, remove them)
1 chipotle (smoke-dried jalapeño), ground or chopped roughly
10 g (¼ oz) cracked black pepper

Weigh the cabbage and determine the salt measurement. Transfer the cabbage to a large bowl or container, sprinkle over the salt and let sit. Pound or massage to get all of the juices out – ideally enough so that if you pick up a handful of cabbage you'll have dripping water flowing from a clenched fist. Add the other ingredients and mix thoroughly. Pack tightly into your jar or crock and weigh down. Seal with your preferred system. Wait. Check. Refrigerate when ready – usually 2–3 weeks, but longer if you like it cured and more complex.

This will keep in the fridge for up to 12 months.

A wonderful way to spend a day with friends is to organise a 'mob-krauting'. The rhythm of grating cabbages with a large wooden shredder into a wooden barrel, salting and stomping the cabbages with a large pounder, or massaging with many hands or little clean feet, adding the spices, jamming it all into a barrel to ferment, to be collected and jarred again in a month or so feels as old and homely as chopping wood.

If you think you'll do this annually, get yourself a large wooden grater, and a large wooden barrel. For fermenting that amount you could buy a large plastic fermenter – with air-lock system – from a home brewer's shop. They are often white, so put it in a dark place to

ferment. Everyone can bring a large jar and take it home packed and ready to ferment, or come back when the kraut is ready, to fill a jar for their fridge.

LOVING YOUR KRAUTS & EATING THEM TOO — SOME IDEAS

Obviously (or not) you can add your ferments to any meal. Just a small amount can transform the flavour of a dish, particularly when it includes fatty elements like cheese or meat, and starchy foods like rice or potato. (Or sweet and oily foods, too.) The acids cut down the fat and make it more digestible. Older culinary cultures like those of Japan and France do this as part of daily life –

a small ferment or pickle takes its place with any normal meal. Just blob a bit on the side of your plate, or in your sandwich. Pretty soon you'll be adding it to eggs, avocado toast or to a bed of rice. It actually comes pretty naturally.

In addition to the recipes and suggestions given here, there are obviously myriad meals you can add your fermented vegies to. If you are eating a fermented food for its probiotics alone, and don't get a lot of ferments in your diet, then keep them raw, otherwise there's no harm in cooking ferments now and then. Personally, I like to keep them raw (seems a waste otherwise), but room temperature, or slightly warmed, is fine.

TRADITIONAL SAUERKRAUT (PAGE 36) LOVES:

— Reuben sandwiches (page 47)

— cheese and ham or salami toasties

— crackers and cheese

— a pile of kraut, with a dash of olive oil and a fried egg on top, with a side of avocado

— dips and dressings (use the juice instead of lime juice in guacamole or in any dressing)

— a juicy sausage in bread with mustard

— mashed potato (stirred through)

— leafy salad (mixed through)

— baked potato with some Labneh (page 111) or cheese (pile it on).

DANISH-INSPIRED RED KRAUT (PAGE 40) LOVES:

— apple: melt some butter, add a peeled and grated or julienned apple and cook until the apple is soft; let it cool to room temperature and then mix the red kraut through the softened apple; serve it up with salty pork chops

— potato salad: boil or steam some potatoes until tender; cool to room temperature, peel and chop, then stir through olive oil, salt and pepper; add some red kraut and crème fraîche or something similar

— smoked trout: add some to the above potato salad; serve with some greens for a complete meal

— crackers with Labneh (page 111) or finely sliced hard cheese

— salad (mixed through)

— sausages.

SMOKY JALAPEÑO KRAUT (PAGE 42) LOVES:

— sweet potato: pile kraut onto a baked sweet potato with butter, a squeeze of lime and Crème fraîche or Labneh (pages 111+112)

— crackers and mild cheese

— fish tacos: to a soft tortilla, add crumbed or fried white fish, sliced or mashed avocado, a squeeze of lime and a blob of kraut

— cheesy omelettes (serve alongside)

— salad (on top with olive oil dribbled over)

— steak

— guacamole (mixed through)

— cheese toasties.

ALL KRAUTS LOVE:

— eggs any style

— avocado

— Labneh (page 111)

— rice and sesame dressing

— potatoes any style – rösti, mashed, baked, stirred through mashed potato and fried up, or beside a scallop potato

— cauliflower soup

— sausages (of course)

— anything creamy or fatty begs for the lovely acidic cut of a good fresh kraut.

I recently had the rare and unexpected experience of having a few of my past and present besties – all from different countries (hard to achieve!) – at my house for a few hours. It was a bit last-minute, but luckily I had three of our favourite krauts in the fridge so I

could show off what I'd been up to lately, just by pairing them with labneh and thin crackers. We served pomegranate water kefir with Aperol on ice, as well as Smreka (page 154) with a local vermouth. Every now and then through a mouthful of food someone would ask me, 'Wait! Did you make this one? Is this yours?' (Seriously I was glowing, both from the joy of seeing my friends, but also at showing them my ferments).

Even with little bites of fermented foods the memories and cravings for more linger; they are a great way to quietly introduce fermented foods. Small, bite-sized amounts are often the best way to consume ferments anyway. Really, a cracker with kraut on it, maybe with a bit of cheese, is enough. Simple as that.

Roger's reuben

The first time Roger and I ever sat down to chat was because he was about to start making reubens at the restaurant he was looking after and wanted to use my kraut. I insisted he add one of my pickles on the side, and thousand island dressing for dipping. That's how I had first loved it years ago at The Tokyo American Club (my haven the second time I lived in Japan with my girls). That was before we'd even set foot into our Jewish neighbourhood of Highland Park, outside Chicago. I know a good reuben and this is it – every part is important, but if you have dry bread for example, at least you'll have the dressing to dip into, right? We often serve these at markets or workshops and they always get rave reviews. Best if you have a sandwich press, but if not, fry your reuben on the stovetop, then pop into the oven to melt the cheese a little.

Roger has written this recipe for four reubens, but we rarely make only four. Make more for cooking later – sit them well covered in the fridge for people to heat up in the sandwich press whenever they like. You can make them a day ahead; just place the kraut in between the cheese and meat to avoid soggy bread.

SERVES: 4

8 slices sourdough, preferably light rye
about 150 g (5½ oz) butter, softened
about 8 slices jarlsberg, gouda or Swiss cheese
about 200 g (7 oz) sauerkraut
dijon mustard (or your own mustard)
12 slices corned beef or pastrami (the thinner the better, and more if you like)
pickles, to serve

THOUSAND ISLAND DRESSING
1 egg yolk
50 g (1¾ oz) dijon mustard
100 ml (3½ fl oz) vinegar
500 ml (17 fl oz/2 cups) olive oil or good-quality vegetable oil
50 ml (1¾ fl oz) tomato sauce (ketchup)
50 ml (1¾ fl oz) worcestershire sauce
healthy pinch of paprika
pinch of chilli flakes
1 tablespoon finely chopped parsley
juice of 1 lemon, to taste

To make the thousand island dressing, place the egg yolk, mustard and a quarter of the vinegar in a food processor or blender and turn the speed to medium.

Slowly drizzle in the oil, ensuring that the mixture combines – you may need to stop pouring occasionally to allow the oil to emulsify with the egg. Keep drizzling until half the oil has been used, then add the rest of the vinegar and blend. Continue to add the oil slowly, and when all of the oil is in and there is no sign of separation, turn the processor or blender off.

Add the sauces, paprika, chilli flakes and parsley, season with salt and pepper and

combine using a spatula. Add lemon juice to taste. Set aside.

Lay out the slices of bread, with top and bottom slices matching in shape and size as best as possible, and butter them all generously, leaving enough butter for the exterior sides of the bread.

Lay the cheese on each of the buttered bread slices, and apply the dijon mustard on one side to taste (I like a lot). Arrange the kraut (make it pretty generous) on the opposite slice.

Place the slices of meat over the mustard. (You can add salt and pepper at this point, but keep in mind that the kraut and meat are salted.)

Close the sandwiches carefully and press together. Apply butter to the top side, turn the sandwich over and butter the other side.

Warm a sandwich press or frying pan to medium–high. Place the reubens in the press, or if frying in a pan, flatten with a spatula.

When the sandwiches are ready, the outside should be golden brown and crisp and the inside warm and the cheese melting. This should take about 5–8 minutes. If cooking from chilled, set the temperature on the press to medium and cook slower, allowing the centre to heat up gradually.

Remove, slice, and place on a warm plate, with a generous dollop of thousand island dressing and a pickle on the side.

Notes: *With the thousand island dressing, you're basically making a delicious mayonnaise … omit the strong flavours and that's what you have. You could then add chopped pickles, capers and parsley and you would have a tartare sauce. Add worcestershire sauce, tomato sauce (ketchup) and lemon juice and you have a cocktail sauce – there are endless varieties of mayonnaise.*

DON'T STOP AT REUBENS FOR SANDWICH IDEAS. TRY THESE TOO:

— Smoky jalapeño kraut (page 42) and a sharp cheese

— Beet red kraut (page 42) with a milky soft cheese like mozzarella, or even a mild blue

— Danish-inspired red kraut (page 40) on rye or wholegrain bread toasted with sardines and kefir Labneh (page 111) or cream cheese.

Kimchi

I'm worried that kimchi is a bit of a fad with the foodies. Don't let that happen to you. It isn't a fad in Korea – it's a staple, eaten at every meal. We don't do that, but I love kimchi because it is basically a meal in a jar, and if you've not much in your fridge except a hefty jar of it, you can have a fabulous dinner. And I needn't go into the health benefits of kimchi – it goes without saying that fermented garlic, ginger and vegetables are good not just in your mouth, but within you, in

KOREAN CHILLI FLAKES (GOCHUGARU)

every way. Koreans have theories on how many illnesses it keeps away or holds at bay.

This is the place to start your kimchi journey if you haven't already, and perhaps on the way you'll gain some confidence. I'm sharing my family favourite that, no kidding, has since become loved by so many on a retail level that we struggle to keep up with production. Once you've made it, or bought it (let's be honest, I know you won't always make it) you won't look back. Kimchi can be found in most countries now, at your Asian grocer or health food shop, if not in your mainstream shop. Check the ingredients for unnecessary preservatives or starter cultures. Don't buy kraut and kimchi that has citric acid listed in the ingredients, and certainly don't buy it if it has been pasteurised and is sitting on a shelf. It needs to be raw and refrigerated and preferably in a glass jar, as the acidity can easily pull chemicals from plastic jars and containers.

The very day you make kimchi you can keep some to eat fresh, like a salad, or in a stir-fry or fried rice. You can eat it at every stage of fermentation – it actually ferments ready to enjoy within a few days to a week.

Slowly fermenting your kimchi somewhere between 5–10°C (41–50°F) for two to three weeks results in a very tasty kimchi, so cooler temperatures are ideal. But the duration depends on personal preference. Taste as you go and when you feel it's ready, jar it up and put it in the fridge. If you leave it out in the cooler months, and it gets more on the sour side, don't worry. Traditionally, older kimchi is used in stews or soups. There's a lovely sourness about year-old kimchi that I love but rarely get, because we almost always eat it all before it gets that old.

There are as many recipes for kimchi as there are opinions on how it should taste. You know how families have secret ingredients, and regions have their specialties? Once you've found your favourite recipe and made it a few times, you can pretty much predict the flavour hit you are going to get. Try to be as consistent as possible by reducing the variables – the temperature, vessels, ingredients and fermenting time. And put your heart into it … I know this sounds corny but food tastes a lot better when you do that; when it's missing, you can't quite put your finger on what it is that's wrong. It tastes flat or something. Perhaps that's the reason people think so fondly of their own mum's kimchi recipe and technique – the memories of kimchi and love meant just for them (okay, I'm corny).

After love, you need the freshest ingredients. Your wombok (Chinese cabbage) should be firm and alive, strong across its body and heavy. Never floppy. It's traditional to make kimchi heading into winter. The vegies are better then, they are tighter and juicier from being in the cold ground. The lower temperatures of early winter support a slower ferment, which will in turn give you more complex and deeper flavours. Having said all that, we make it any time of year and always love it. I'm just being posh and pedantic about the winter thing …

YOU SHOULD HAVE:

THE CHILLI FLAKES (GOCHUGARU)

Real Korean chilli is very important for a good kimchi, as every Korean will tell you. It has a long, gentle warmth, rather than a quick spicy hit. It's worth your time making a trip to your local Korean or Asian food shop to source this because it makes all the difference. Normal chilli powder will not have the same smoky flavours, or colour, and will be spicier than Korean chilli. If you only have normal chilli,

then add less than my recipe recommends. Or ... if no gochugaru? White kimchi is a thing too (see page 60). It's Korea's oldest and original kimchi and has no chilli at all – more like a sauerkraut. We call it 'Kid-chi' for the kids who come over and are a bit shy about eating chilli. I won't tell a lie: I'm not patient with fussiness, and always plan to build them up to liking the spicy one ... but you have got to start somewhere.

THE KIMCHI PASTE

The most important thing after fresh ingredients and love is the kimchi paste. Many recipes implore you to source the best ingredients. In my mind, you should make your own kimchi paste using real Korean chilli flakes, as I mentioned, and a good fish sauce at least.

Fish sauce! For me, until recently, it was a small bottle in the back of the cupboard used for stir-fries and splashed into a dish here and there. It's no wonder nobody really likes it, because most of the supermarket stuff isn't fermented, and certainly has a lot of added ingredients. True fish sauce is actually supposed to be purely salt and fish. And time. Like two years. A good fish sauce is sweet and mild, and you could almost drink a little shot glass of it. Please hunt a bottle of this down for your cupboard and for your kimchi. And while you're at it, get the best soy sauce you can find, as it has its own highly commercialised problems as well.

In each of the following recipes, you can add as much chilli as you desire, even doubling the amount if you like it hot.

Also! Make a double portion of the paste if you can be bothered, because this is great to keep in a jar in the fridge for next time. You could take some from that jar for all kinds of other things, like stir fries, or to add some to rice or a beef marinade, for example. You can even add a small amount to your cucumber pickles (see page 69) or to a dressing or mayonnaise.

(One) recipe for kimchi (baechu kimchi)

There are many different recipes for kimchi, so keep your mind open and feel free to add or take away as your taste buds dictate – this is a 'ferm' favourite.

Preparation time: 2 hours–overnight
Fermentation time: 5+ normal days or 3 hot days
Equipment: 2 L (68 fl oz) jar, pounder (optional), your chosen lidding system

2 wombok (Chinese cabbages)
5–6 tablespoons salt
65 g (2¼ oz/1 cup) sliced spring onions (scallions)
155 g (5½ oz/1 cup) grated daikon (white radish)
155 g (5½ oz/1 cup) grated carrot
1–2 nashi pears, sliced (optional; see notes)

Kimchi paste

4 garlic bulbs or 20–40 peeled garlic cloves (see notes)
500 g (1 lb 2 oz) fresh ginger, unpeeled
1 cup gochugaru (Korean chilli flakes)
125 ml (4 fl oz/½ cup) fish sauce (see notes)
110 g (4 oz/½ cup) organic raw (demerara) sugar (see notes)
125 ml (4 fl oz/½ cup) tamari or light soy sauce

Remove and discard the outer leaves of the wombok if they are damaged or discoloured. Wash the wombok, slice lengthways into quarters, then chop these lengths into bite-sized pieces. Place the chopped wombok into a large bowl, sprinkle with the salt and mix well. Let it sit for a few hours, or even overnight if you've room in your fridge.

Blend the kimchi paste ingredients (minus the sugar if you're adding the pears) into a paste.

Drain the cabbage, add the other vegetables (and the pears if you omitted the sugar from the paste) and mix your paste through the vegetables well. You may want to put some gloves on for this, because you really need to get in there and mix it all in and around.

You could keep this in the bowl, covered, to ferment, but I prefer to jar it. Push the vegetables down quite firmly with your fist or a pounder. You should easily have enough juice to cover all of the vegetables, so you won't need to weigh them down (see notes about headroom). Seal with your chosen lidding system (see from page 26).

Leave the jar on your bench for a few days. It should start to come alive, and if you happen to be using an air-lock system then you'll be lucky enough to hear it bubble.

Pop it in the fridge after 5 normal days or 3 hot days; go longer if it's cool in your house or you like it mature. You could even put the crock or jar in the fridge to ferment from day 1 and leave it there to ferment for about 3 weeks. If you fridge-ferment you can add less salt. Add a touch more salt in hot weather.

This will keep for a long time in your fridge and will keep getting sourer with age.

Notes: *It's okay to omit the sugar and replace with 1–2 sliced nashi pears.*

It's a lot of garlic to peel – make it easier by putting the individual cloves into a bowl and covering it with a similar sized bowl and shaking it like crazy to shake the skin off. Shake it hard though.

Make sure the fish sauce is REAL. Check the ingredients – they should only include fish (anchovies) and salt.

When I talk to you of headroom, I'm serious and you need to pay attention. Don't push it! Kimchi will produce gas and liquid as it ferments. You really are better off either getting another smaller jar to ferment leftovers in, or just cook it up or throw it out. Whatever you do, don't be too optimistic and fill the jar all the way. Leave some room in your crock or jar, or it will overflow. Best to use an air-lock system for kimchi, but even then, if you don't leave headroom the liquid will spill out of the air-lock and you'll have red liquid everywhere. If it's a warm day it may do this quicker than you'd expect.

When our kimchi started becoming a thing, and was ordered by shops in larger quantities, we became a little overwhelmed. We first started making it in 4 litre (135 fl oz) jars, and then upgraded to a 15 litre (4 gallon) German crock. Next, we moved to 50 litre (13 gallon) food-grade plastic fermenters with air-locks.

Late one kimchi-making night, we had a bit left over and didn't want to have a tub only a quarter full, so we just filled the tubs all the way. Just two days later I thought I'd better go and put them in the fridge as it had been hot and I was worried they'd ferment too quickly. When I got to The Fermentary there was red kimchi juice spewing out of the air traps and pooling into the lids. The floors were covered in red. Naturally we decided to open them straight away to see if they were okay.

Wendy and I tried to open the vats and couldn't. They were jammed up tight. I ended up wrapping my arms and legs around one vat, bum almost to the ground, hugging it tightly as Wendy tried to open it. Grunting and tugging, trying to unscrew the lid, we started wondering how we'd get them open when finally, the pressure literally BLEW the lid off and the kimchi BURST out of the vat like a volcano spewing red spicy liquid up into the air, into Wendy's face and down all over me. Not just a little bit – half the vat kept bursting up and out. The first vat was a shock and we were dismayed by the amount of time and work we'd put into making it … all of those orders for next week, all of the cleaning, no kimchi for anyone, just mess to clean up. The worst part was when we went to open the next barrel and realised its lid was also tight – and so was the next and the next. The four other over-filled vats were equally explosive, but we just had to take the eruption one vat at a time. If either Wendy or I were into Instagram at the time, I don't think we'd have even been able to take a photo, we were so distraught. We had orders we couldn't fill and had spent money and time on those barrels of kimchi. So listen up kids, and always leave headroom. If it gets too hot, move your ferment into a cooler place. We smelled of garlic for days after that, which helped get us back into the kitchen because, actually, the smell of kimchi is good enough to bring anyone back.

Whole kimchi (tongbaechu kimchi)

This is a traditional way to make kimchi. It not only looks quite beautiful but is great because you can pull the cabbage out and chop it to the size you'd like. You can make lovely perfectly layered squares, or chop it finely for adding to another dish. It's up to you. Pulling it from the vat whole is … memorable, I think.

Adding raw seafood, such as oysters, is common, particularly on the southern tip of South Korea, which makes sense, being near the ocean. If you decide to add seafood, because you are adding it raw and it's going to ferment, make sure it's fresh and of high quality. Clean it in a salt water bath and drain before using. The seafood is best added to small batches that you'll ferment in the fridge and eat up pretty quickly.

Preparation time: 2 hours
Fermentation time: 3+ days
Equipment: large crock or jar, your chosen lidding system

3 wombok (Chinese cabbages)

DRY BRINING
65 g (2¼ oz/½ cup) salt

NORMAL BRINING
about 630 g (1 lb 6 oz/2 cups) good coarse sea salt (calculate the percentage based on the weight of the cabbage; see method)
about 2.5 litres (85 fl oz) water

KIMCHI PASTE
500 ml (17 fl oz/2 cups) water
2 tablespoons (sweet) glutinous rice flour
2 tablespoons sugar
1–2 garlic bulbs, peeled and crushed (use less garlic if you don't love it, more if you do)
2.5 cm (1 in) piece of fresh ginger, finely grated
200 ml (7 fl oz) good fish sauce
1–2 cups Korean chilli flakes (gochugaru)
½ onion, peeled
2 carrots, peeled and julienned
1 small daikon (white radish), peeled and julienned
5 spring onions (scallions), sliced

Trim the bottom of the wombok and cut them down the middle halfway, enough so that you can pull the cabbage gently apart. Then cut a small slit in the bottom, just to open the bases up a bit, but keeping them together.

To dry brine (which takes less time), dip the cabbages in clean cold water and then sprinkle the salt all over, making sure you get salt in between the leaves. Pile the cabbages together and leave them to sit for 2 hours, flipping and turning them every half hour. They may need some more time depending on the temperature. They should be shrinking and producing more water after each 30 minute period.

To brine in the normal way, immerse the cabbages in a clean sink in a 15–20% brine (use the amounts in the ingredient list as a guide for this), using something like a large plate to keep the cabbages under the brine. You can leave them overnight or for a few hours. The cabbages are ready when you can bend a leaf backwards without breaking it. Whatever method you use, when the cabbages are ready, wash and drain a few times, and then gently pull them apart into quarters.

After rinsing well, have a taste. It will be saltier than you'd like to eat, but not too salty. If you think it is too salty, rinse again.

To make the kimchi paste, first heat the water in a saucepan over low heat. Add the rice flour until it's paste-like, stirring to avoid lumps.

Add the sugar and keep stirring until dissolved. This will thicken your kimchi paste so it stays on and within the cabbage, rather than drip down and away from it.

Blitz the garlic, ginger, fish sauce, chilli flakes and onion in a blender and add to the flour mixture, stirring to combine.

Mix the carrot, daikon and spring onion into the paste.

Now take your drained wombok and remove the hard core at the end. Then wipe each layer with the kimchi paste, smearing it between the leaves, making sure the entire cabbage has paste on and in it. Fold each piece as you finish and place into your crock or jar, or even a BPA-free food-grade plastic container. Pack down tightly so there are no air pockets, put on the lid and let it sit. A couple of days later, check it – upon pushing down there should be a lot more liquid, and it should have started fermenting. If it's bubbling, you'll know it has started. You can let it go for a couple more days, or pop it into a root cellar or fridge to ferment slowly for longer. It will keep in the fridge for months, getting sourer with time.

Note: *This is delicious cut neatly and topped with its juices and toasted sesame seeds. Or you can chop it up and add it to soups and other cooked dishes.*

White 'kid-chi' (baek kimchi)

White kimchi is actually thought to be the original Korean kimchi. The chilli didn't come until later on. It seems that all around the world at around the same time everyone was making a white cabbage ferment. Crazy, huh?

We initially made it for visiting children who were a bit turned off by the idea of spice, but it turned out to be so delicious, with so much texture, it was no longer just for kids! You can leave out any of the ingredients that might be hard on them or hard to find, without any problems.

Preparation time: 2 hours–overnight
Fermentation time: 3 days
Equipment: muslin (cheesecloth), large crock or jar, your chosen lidding system

2 generous tablespoons salt (see page 59 for additional salt quantity needed for the normal brining method)
1 litre (34 fl oz/4 cups) water
about 1.5 kg (3 lb 5 oz) wombok (Chinese cabbage)
½ daikon (white radish), scrubbed or peeled; then julienned or finely sliced
1 carrot, peeled and julienned; or in fine rounds
3 spring onions (scallions), chopped
2 jujubes (also known as Chinese or red dates), pitted and finely sliced
2–3 dried shiitake mushrooms, finely sliced (optional; see notes)
2–4 fresh raw (peeled) chestnuts or water chestnuts, finely sliced (optional; see notes)
2 tablespoons salt

KIMCHI PASTE
1 nashi pear
5 garlic cloves, peeled
½ onion, peeled
1 thumb-sized piece of fresh ginger

Make a jug or deep bowl of brine by dissolving the 2 generous tablespoons of salt into the water.

Make the kimchi paste by blitzing all the ingredients in a blender. Transfer the paste to a piece of muslin, tie with a knot and dangle it into the brine so the flavour infuses. You can do this a day before if you like, but let sit for at least a couple of hours. Remove the muslin package.

Wash and prepare the wombok using the normal brining method in the Whole kimchi recipe on page 59.

Mix the daikon, carrot, spring onion, jujube, mushrooms and chestnuts (if using) together with the extra 2 teaspoons of salt and gently spread the mixture between each cabbage leaf. Fold each cabbage leaf in half over itself as you go. Place each cabbage into your crock or jar; a deep long glass baking dish can be used if you don't have a crock. Layer the cabbages on top of each other, or if in a dish then side by side, and then pour the brine over the top to cover. Seal with a lid and sit at room temperature for a few days. Check after the third day and if it's sour enough for you, put it into the fridge. It will last about 6 weeks.

Notes: *I add shiitake mushroom because I love the chewy texture and the flavour it gives the brine.*

Water chestnuts are easier to find than raw chestnuts – even the tinned kind are fine to use – and make a lovely, crunchy addition.

Serve as you would your regular kimchi, keeping in mind that the flavour is fresher, more like sauerkraut. It goes well as a side with other spicy food and also with rice topped with black and white sesame seeds.

LOVING YOUR KIMCHI & EATING IT TOO — SOME IDEAS

Kimchi juice

When you have a large batch of kimchi and you want to jar it into smaller ones, you'll find there's a heap of juice at the bottom of your barrel. Bottle it! This is beautiful juice that can be used as a marinade, in dressings, fried rice, guacamole, and most popular of all, in bloody marys. Amounts will depend on your taste, and you may want to strain it first. It's also fantastic as a shot for gut health. My daughter Lulu easily drinks a full 250 ml (8½ fl oz/1 cup) of this in one go when she's in the mood – which is a couple of times a week – and therefore that sweet little girl often gets some serious garlic breath action happening. Oh well.

Kimchi with pork belly, herbs & lime

The perfect use of a ferment (aside from eating it with friends) is to serve it with fatty foods. Fat with an acid! There's so much good about the silky soft pork belly and the warm acidic crunch of kimchi; it's had its time as our go-to for visitors and workshops. This is an easy one to cook for a lot of people because you only need a small piece of pork belly each. It's a cinch to cook, and you made the kimchi maybe a month ago, right?

MAKES: 8 SMALL PORTIONS (A SMALL SERVE IS ALL YOU NEED OF PORK BELLY)

2–3 kg (4 lb 6 oz–6 lb 10 oz) pork belly, deboned
olive oil, to rub and drizzle
handful of sea salt flakes
freshly ground black pepper, to taste

>>> *continued on page 64*

kimchi, to serve
1 bunch of Thai basil, leaves picked
1 bunch of coriander (cilantro), leaves picked
1 bunch of flat-leaf (Italian) parsley,
    leaves picked
6 spring onions (scallions), chopped on an angle
1 or 2 long chillies, seeds and membranes
    removed, cut into thin strips
3 limes
1 tablespoon sesame seeds

Preheat the oven to 220°C (430°F).

Pat the pork belly dry with paper towel and score the skin in a criss-cross pattern with a sharp knife or blade. Rub with olive oil and scatter the salt and pepper over the skin, rubbing in thoroughly, making sure to get it into the cut sections.

Transfer to a baking tray and roast for 30 minutes. Drop the temperature to 150°C (300°F) and slow roast for 2–3 more hours, or until the pork belly is tender by touch. This will depend on its size.

Allow to cool on a rack for 15 minutes.

Once the pork is cooked, I like to remove the pork skin/crackling and give it another blast in the oven to ensure a nice crunch. Do that if you wish, and while the skin's crisping up, cut the belly into portion sizes and transfer them to serving plates.

Spoon a generous amount of kimchi on top of the belly, or to the side if you'd prefer. Combine the herbs, spring onion and chilli in a bowl and arrange a tuft on top of each portion. Drizzle with olive oil and a squeeze of lime juice and sprinkle with the sesame seeds.

Serve the pork crackling on the side, or crumble it over the top.

Roger's chilli chicken

This is Roger's go-to to please the kids. If they walk through the door and we are having chilli chicken, they all celebrate. We also lean on this dish when we have a crowd of people over. Parents of the children who've been at our place and eaten it ask Roger to make it for them because their kids have come home and raved about it. He has to stand at the deep-fryer for a while, which I think must be annoying, but it's outside, and I think he likes the escape. No complaints from him, the repetition looks quite comforting and everyone is happy.

In Roger's words: I've been doing this recipe for 20 years and people love it like crazy. Once you get it down pat you can do it all very quickly. Kids love it, but there is a bit of a kick from the kimchi paste, so be aware.

SERVES: 6–8

1.5 kg (3 lb 5 oz) chicken leg quarters, boned
    and skinned (see notes)
345 g (12 oz/1½ cups) caster (superfine) sugar
    (see notes)
200 g (7 oz) kimchi paste (see notes or page 55)
600 g (4¾ cups/1 lb 2 oz) cornflour (cornstarch)
canola oil, for deep-frying

Cut the chicken into finger-sized strips.

Combine the sugar and the kimchi paste and season with salt and pepper.

Coat the chicken strips in the mixture. It's best to do this the day before (and store, covered, in the fridge), but I have done it 30 minutes before and it's been fine.

Pour the cornflour into a double-layered plastic bag. Add a couple of handfuls of the marinated chicken to the bag and shake. The chicken strips need to separate and be coated in cornflour. Make sure you shake off the excess as you remove the chicken from the bag. Continue with this until all the chicken is coated in cornflour.

Heat the deep-fryer and carefully and quickly place the strips in one or two at a time and deep-fry until golden brown. Don't add too much to the fryer at once or the oil will cool down.

Keep the chicken warm in the oven while you fry the remaining strips. Season with salt when you serve.

Notes: *I like chicken leg meat as it has more flavour and retains moisture, but you can use breast.*

If you don't have any kimchi paste, you can pop some kimchi into a blender and blitz it. If you don't have any kimchi to pop into a blender, just use 1 teaspoon of cayenne pepper as this gives the heat. Use less if you have kids who are unsure about spice.

This recipe does not work without sugar. The sugar and cornflour form the crunchy exterior.

I serve the chicken with a salad of cucumber, tomato and coriander (cilantro); roasted cubed sweet potato topped with yoghurt and spring onion (scallion); steamed rice; chilli sauce; sweet soy sauce (kecap manis); Tzatziki (page 96); and Japanese sesame mayo.

MORE EASY IDEAS FOR USING YOUR KIMCHI

Kimchi enhances many foods, but particularly eggs cooked in any way (I wish more places had kimchi on the menu for breakfast), avocado, sesame seeds or tahini, cheese, sweet potatoes, potatoes and, of course, rice. On top of these staple combos, here are a few more ideas.

— Kimchi goes GREAT in toasted sandwiches. Use any bread, with butter on the outside, add cheese (or tahini instead of cheese) and kimchi and toast in a sandwich press.

— Mix tahini through kimchi and eat it as a side, or on some noodles or rice cakes for a snack.

— Blob some tahini in the kimchi jar and eat it from the jar – tahini and kimchi love each other.

— Pile it in a 'Buddha bowl' – rice or a grain with kimchi, avocado, sesame seeds, sesame dressing and a poached egg.

— Incorporate kimchi into an omelette mixture, or serve alongside.

— Bake a sweet potato, halve it, and put kimchi, sesame dressing and mayo on top.

— Dish up a bowl of rice with a bit of sesame oil and black sesame seeds, little sausages, a fried egg and kimchi.

— Serve on steamed rice with Japanese mayonnaise and sesame dressing.

— Top a piece of toasted nori with kimchi as a snack.

— Make a kimchi steamed bun and serve with some greens and a piece of pork belly.

— Use in sushi (with some cream cheese, chicken, sesame seeds and avocado).

— Put kimchi over hot chips with some melted cheese.

— Chop some kimchi and mix it through nattō (page 186).

— Use kimchi juice as a marinade; add it to dressings, soaking liquids, 'Fire tonic' (page 158), and bloody marys.

Brine & dry salt ferments

Those pickles you buy on the shelf from the shops aren't lacto-fermented. They are preserved – which is great, and they are tasty. But they are pretty much devoid of life because they are preserved in vinegar, and heated to kill any life that might make them dangerous. This is useful, because it's a way of storing food for years. Done correctly, no bacteria or mould will come and invade your food. Buy those, and make those, but don't pretend they are the same as a wild brine ferment. They aren't. And the flavour is very different. The sour taste in them comes from vinegar.

Wild brine ferments are the real 'dill' (sorry). The sour comes from lactic acid, and the flavours are complex and earthy, and they feel amazing as they hit your belly. You know they are good for your gut, so it's pretty normal (and particularly satisfying) to see a whole jar of carrots or beans eaten in one sitting.

This is lacto-fermentation at its easiest. Once you experience how easy brine fermenting is, you won't hesitate to grab some vegies and whip them into a life-giving preservation. The flavour combinations are endless here. Use my recipes as a guide; the amounts can be changed depending on how much you have or can fit into your jar or crock. Keep the salt percentage around the same though.

Just as with the krauts, no oxygen is allowed in this environment; direct sunlight is not the best; and when you reach your desired, perfect flavour point, all you need to do is slow it down in the fridge. I prefer to use an air-lock system, but a flip-top jar – one with rubber rings and a clip – would work too because it releases gases. A normal jar is fine, just let the gas out by opening it quickly every day or so.

WATER

The water you use for your ferments should be filtered or unchlorinated. If your tap water is full of chemicals, then boil it or leave it out in an open container overnight.

SALT

Salt content is important, as usual, and in brining, we use salt on its own to either draw out water (as with lemons), or in a brine with water and herbs and spices. The amount of salt you need for brining is different to when you ferment krauts – too much salt will inhibit the lactic acid bacteria, which we actually want; too little and your vegetable might go soggy. Your salt content will depend on how dense your vegetable is – softer ones like cucumbers require more salt (we use a 7% brine) than beets, for example, which I recommend you ferment in a 3% brine.

MAKING THE BRINE

With brines I have to admit to being a bit relaxed and that is fine – no need to be too pedantic. A lazy way to make one is to place the salt in the jar first, then add all of your other ingredients, pour the water over, lid it and give the whole

thing a good shake to dissolve the salt. (This works pretty well with fine salt, but if you are using a coarse salt, best to dissolve it first.) Add the follower and weights after shaking.

Otherwise, make your brine by dissolving the salt into a small amount of hot water first, then add the rest of the water, stir, and pour into your jars or crock.

HEADROOM

Just as with krauts and kimchi, you'll need to leave headroom and room for your weights. For cut vegetables, be sure to cut them evenly and to the right length to fit the jar.

FOLLOWER & WEIGHT

A follower is important because sometimes the vegetables float to the top when you want them to stay under the brine. Find a good system to hold them down, or shove the vegetables in so tightly that a simple grape leaf or folded cabbage leaf becomes a kind of barrier to hold them down. Something that fits nice and snug is good.

For a weight, you can use another smaller jar that fits snugly enough to push the vegetables down and let the brine rise up to cover. With this method, be sure to use a cloth to keep dust and bugs away. If you don't mind plastic then a zip-lock bag filled with pie weights, marbles or even brine works pretty well too. Using another vegetable chunk cut to the size you need is pretty lovely – carrots are perfect for this.

VEGETABLES

Brine fermenting is best done with firm vegies. High chlorophyll, very seedy or soft vegetables are all best preserved using another method – ones that don't do well are kale, basil and lettuce, for example. If you must brine ferment with those, perhaps chop them up and make them into salsas or pastes, such as pesto, first. This works well, and ferments quite quickly. But it's not my favourite.

Give your vegetables a quick wash before you ferment them, but not too vigorously, as the skins may carry good bacteria that we need.

FLAVOURS

Adding spice is easy and completely up to you, but try to stick to three flavours that generally go together. Don't crush your spices – keep them whole to limit mould. If you are planning on only doing a three-day ferment, then this isn't such a problem – crush them to get to the flavour faster.

If you want to use herbs such as coriander (cilantro) and parsley, use the root or stem part that holds all the flavour – the leaves can get soggy or slimy. Reserve the leaves for dishes that aren't fermented.

The amounts depend on the jar size of course, but it's better to be subtle rather than overbearing. A thin slice of lemon zest is always lovely. A good combination is a herb, a seed or two, and an allium.

The below combinations are some of my favourites, but just recommendations:

— garlic, chilli and black pepper

— dill, mustard seeds and garlic

— lemon zest, garlic and chilli

— lemongrass, coriander seeds and chilli

— mustard seeds, chopped shallot and a sprig of thyme or tarragon

— dill and parsley root, fennel seeds and orange zest

— turmeric, pepper and chilli

— ginger, coriander seed or root and garlic

— celery seeds, caraway seeds, juniper berries and garlic

— star anise, bay leaf and pepper.

TO FERMENT

Keep your jar out of any direct sunlight and at a constant room temperature of 14–21°C (57–70°F). I like to keep mine on the bench to watch and listen to the bubbles. Fermenting time will depend on the vegetable and how warm it is in your kitchen, etc. The harder the vegetable the longer it'll take. After about three days the liquid might turn cloudy, which is normal, and there could be a funky discolouration at the top. That's okay. Taste some and if it's suitably sour, then put it into the fridge to slow any further fermenting right down. Keep the vegetables under the brine. Enjoy! Hopefully they'll taste sour and good and you won't be able to stop at one. These ferments will keep in the fridge for at least six months.

The REAL dill (pickle)

We want these cucumbers to retain their crunch, so it's best to look for the gherkin-style cucumbers, which are small but thick-skinned. Regular cucumbers with thin skins are okay, but up the salt content a bit with these to make sure they stay crunchy.

To be honest, I'm not friends with detailed fiddly things and most of my salt measurements for brines are measured by a cupped palmful. (Enough salt for a 1.5 litre/51 fl oz jar is a cupped palmful – or about 2½ tablespoons.) But work out your own method, or measure properly if you prefer.

A very important ingredient for keeping the cucumbers crispy is a bit of tannin. We use fresh grape leaves because we have them, but raspberry, blackberry or oak leaves are good, as are tea leaves (just a few loose leaves from tea you buy will do). If you have enough leaves, put one on the bottom, and then use another leaf as a follower to hold the pickles under the brine before adding a weight, and sealing your vessel.

Preparation time: 15 minutes
Fermentation time: 5+ days
Equipment: 1 L (34 fl oz) jar, ceramic crock or Japanese pickle press (I like to use an air-lock system but any jar will do really), weight

500 g (1 lb 2 oz) small thick-skinned cucumbers
1–2 grape leaves or other tannin-rich leaves (optional but recommended)
2–3 garlic cloves (depending on size), peeled
1 teaspoon mustard seeds
1 tablespoon whole peppercorns (mixed is nice)
1 fresh bird's eye chilli, or 1 teaspoon dried chilli flakes
2–3 fresh dill stalks and fronds, or 2 teaspoons whole dill seeds
2–4 tablespoons good, fine salt (for every 500 ml/17 fl oz/2 cups water, add 1 tablespoon salt)
1–2 litres (34–68 fl oz/4–8 cups) water (best to use rainwater, filtered, or tap water boiled and cooled)

Take the blossom end off the cucumbers as it has enzymes in it that can make the cucumber go soft. The blossom end sticks out more than the stem end, but you can take off both ends if you are confused.

Put a grape leaf in the bottom of your jar, then strategically place the cucumbers on top, squeezing as many in as possible by packing them tightly. Don't allow in any that are spoiled or a bit soft because they won't ferment well.

Add the garlic, mustard seeds, peppercorns, chilli, dill and any other spices you'd like. (You can even omit all of these and stick to simply salt and water.)

Make your brine with the salt and water (see page 66 for more on this) and pour into the jar over the vegetables, using as much as you need to cover them completely.

Top with another leaf if you have one; it will make a great follower to keep the cucumbers under the brine. Top with your chosen weighting system and seal.

Wait 5–10 days, taste and refrigerate.

LOVING YOUR PICKLES & EATING THEM TOO — ONE IDEA

Everybody knows what pickles go with. You just eat them out of the jar, sliced on a hamburger, whole and next to a sandwich, or chopped with mayo and dill in a potato salad. It's actually a thing to slice, batter, deep-fry and serve them with ranch dressing. (Um ... I've never done that.)

I'm not sure if you know about pickles in soups, but you should. Try the recipe below, because trust me: pickles are an amazing addition to soup. There's something about the texture of the pickle – the sour crunch, not cooked, not raw – paired with the brine in the broth that adds a sweet–sour depth and lovely length that is gorgeous.

Lamb shank & pickle soup

I love this soup and so does my family. The sweet and fatty lamb shanks go beautifully with the pickles and the brine. It's crunchy and sweet and sour and smooth and so warming, and the barley is slightly chewy. You could use small pasta or rice if you don't have barley. As you would imagine, this goes really well with a chunk of sourdough and butter. Another tip – have some apple pie with crème fraîche for dessert and you will have the perfect hearty yet refreshing meal.

SERVES: 6

500 g (1 lb 2 oz) lamb shanks
butter and oil, for browning
2.5 litres (85 fl oz) water
2 onions (1 whole for the broth, 1 peeled and diced)
1 bay leaf
1 teaspoon black peppercorns
1 teaspoon juniper berries
110 g (4 oz/½ cup) barley
4 tablespoons ghee
1 small bunch of parsley, chopped (reserve a little for serving)
1 carrot, peeled and finely chopped
1 cup chopped pickles
125 ml (4 fl oz/½ cup) pickle brine
2 spring onions (scallions), chopped finely, to scatter
Danish rye or sourdough, to serve

Brown the shanks in some butter and oil in a frying pan, then transfer to a large stockpot.

Cover with the water. Add the whole onion, bay leaf, peppercorns and juniper berries.

Bring to the boil, then reduce the heat. Skim off the scum that rises to the surface.

Simmer covered for the first hour, then uncovered for a further hour.

When the meat is tender and falling off the bone, pull the shanks from the soup and gently remove the meat.

Remove the onion, bay leaf and spices, or strain the soup.

Put the soup back on the heat, then add the meat and barley. Cook for 15 minutes, or until the barley is cooked but still has a bite.

While that's cooking, heat the ghee in a frying pan and sweat the diced onion. When the onion is translucent, add the parsley and carrot.

Continue to cook, stirring often, until soft and slightly caramelised. Transfer the onion mixture to the soup.

Before serving, add the chopped pickles, taste, then pour in the pickle brine, tasting as you go. If you feel it needs more sour kick then add more brine until you're happy.

By now the broth should taste rich, salty, sour and sweet.

Scatter with spring onion and parsley, and serve with some Danish rye or a good sourdough.

Whole corn on the cob

This was last summer's fad at The Fermentary. As with other ferments, this is slow food that becomes your fast food go-to because you can eat it raw. YES! The corn takes on a slightly sour flavour, is soft enough to eat straight from the barrel, and if you include jalapeño chillies they leave that slightly hot aftertaste. You'll need a 4–5 litre (135–170 fl oz) jar or, even better, a large crock. You could even go and buy a large fermenting tub from a home brew shop for this because it's worth it – especially for a special event, large gathering or barbecue. Trust me. We've made this for markets and it is crazy popular, destined to become an annual celebration of corn.

Preparation time: ↓25 minutes
Fermentation time: 1–2 weeks
Equipment: 4–5 L (135–170 fl oz) jar (or large crock or tub), weight

8–10 corn cobs, peeled, silks removed
5 litres (170 fl oz) water
8 tablespoons salt
10 garlic cloves
3–5 jalapeño chillies, seeds and membranes removed, sliced (if you want more heat, leave the seeds and membranes intact and just halve)
1 tablespoon whole black peppercorns
2 sprigs of parsley, root only, no leaves
2 sprigs of coriander (cilantro), root only, no leaves (don't waste the leaves, use them for something else)

Blanch the corn in some boiling water briefly – 30 seconds will do. We aren't blanching them to cook them, just to break the starch down, damaging the cell walls a bit.

Once blanched, cool the corn down as quickly as possible by putting it straight into the fridge if you have room. Putting it in an iced water bath tends to take away some sweetness and flavour, so avoid that if possible.

You could cut the corn cobs into 5 cm (2 in) pieces, but I love keeping them in one piece. (You'll need a vessel that can fit them whole.)

While the corn is cooling, make your brine straight in your fermenting vessel using the water and salt. You could use some boiling water to dissolve the salt if you like. Add the remaining ingredients to the brine.

Add your cooled whole corn cobs to the vessel. Make sure you have enough brine to cover the corn. Put a weight on, such as a plate, or something to keep the corn under the brine, and seal your jar or crock. Tightly wrapped plastic wrap is fine if you've only got a crock with no lid.

>>> continued on page 74

LEFT: WHOLE CORN ON THE COB (PAGE 71)
BELOW: CARROTS (PAGE 75)

Ferment the corn like this for about a week. Just like other ferments, the longer you leave it, the sourer it will get; if you've got a cool place to put it you could let it go for longer. Otherwise jar it up and put it in the fridge, where it'll stay good and crisp for about 3 months.

Notes: *Ooooh how we love to take the whole tub of corn outside and pull from it directly to cook over coals. We even bought a long narrow barbecue to fit corn perfectly. When we grill over coals we are really only aiming for a quick burn because the sugars are all out on the surface and easy to burn, giving an awesome smoky flavour. It's more of a quick heating compared to a raw cob on the barbecue, because the starches are almost all gone. Slather with your own Kefir cultured butter (page 114) mixed with some lime zest and a bit of chopped coriander (cilantro). So good!*

Try it raw: you don't actually need to cook the corn at all – it's great as a snack, chopped into smaller pieces and put in lunchboxes. Take it off the cob for salsas or salads.

Carrots

Giving a child, or yourself, a fermented carrot stick to snack on is so many levels up on a regular carrot in flavour, and of course in nutritional value. Just like I promised, this is fast slow food ready to grab and eat at any time. All the preparation is done before. Just peel and cut the carrots into rounds or sticks, depending on how you'd like to snack on them. I like rounds because they are bite-sized and perfect for munching on while I'm at the computer or watching TV. Sticks are great for dipping and also to give the kids to take with them as an on-the-run snack – often in the car.

The brine ratio should be roughly 3%.

Preparation time: 5–10 minutes
Fermentation time: 1 week
Equipment: 1 L (34 fl oz) jar, follower, weight

your favourite flavour combination (optional; see page 68)
300 g (10½ oz) carrots (or enough to fill your jar), peeled and chopped
about 2–3 tablespoons fine salt
1 litre (34 fl oz/4 cups) water (or enough to cover your carrots)

Add your favourite flavour combination to the jar if you wish. Fill the jar with the carrots.

Make a brine with the salt and water (see page 66) and pour over the carrots, using as much as you need to cover them completely. Follow and weigh them down (see page 68) and seal the jar.

They are ready to eat when you think they are delicious (about a week). When you've decided they are sour enough, pop them into the fridge for safekeeping. They'll last for months like that.

Green beans

This is another great brine ferment. My kids get these in their lunchboxes. And I also eat them at my desk. I'm eating one now.

Preparation time: 15 minutes
Fermentation time: 3+ days
Equipment: 1 L (34 fl oz) jar

300 g (10½ oz) green beans (or enough to fill your jar nice and tightly), topped and tailed, strings removed
your favourite flavour combination (optional; see note and page 68)
1 litre (34 fl oz/4 cups) water
2 tablespoons fine salt

Pack the beans tightly into the jar. Add your favourite flavour combination, if using.

Make a brine with the water and salt (see page 66) and pour it into the jar, leaving headroom. Seal the jar.

This is a fast ferment – it will only need to ferment for 3–5 days at room temperature. It can go longer – just test and refrigerate before it goes soft. Keep in the fridge for up to 8 weeks.

Note: *My favourite flavour combination with beans or carrots is 1–2 garlic cloves, 1 dill stalk or some fennel and 5 black and red peppercorns.*

Cauliflower

This is one of the stinkiest ferments to open, but surprisingly delicious and a fabulous addition to a charcuterie plate. Cauliflower can take more flavours, which get stronger the longer you leave it. It is regularly paired with curry spices, so go ahead and try that too if you like.

Preparation time: 15 minutes
Fermentation time: 1–6 weeks
Equipment: 2 L (68 fl oz) jar, air-lock system, weight

2 litres (68 fl oz/8 cups) water
4 tablespoons fine salt
1 cauliflower, broken into bite-sized florets
2 garlic cloves, peeled
3 tarragon sprigs
3 dried or fresh bird's eye chillies
2 teaspoons yellow or brown mustard seeds
2 teaspoons coriander seeds
a few black peppercorns
1 vine leaf or another tannin-rich leaf

Make a brine with the water and salt (page 66).
   Pack the cauliflower tightly into the jar, leaving headroom and without breaking the florets. Add the garlic, tarragon, chillies, seeds and peppercorns, then top with the vine leaf.
   Pour the brine over, making sure to cover the contents. Weigh down the cauliflower (see page 68), ensuring it stays under the brine, but leaving headroom – don't fill to the brim.
   To seal, I use an air-lock system for this ferment as it is very active. Let it ferment at room temperature for a week , then seal with a lid and put it into the fridge to keep fermenting a bit longer. Cauliflower is the kind of ferment that could benefit from a 'kimchi fridge' or wine fridge. It could ferment for 6 weeks in a cool place.
   Open and eat. The brine is as good as any and can be taken straight. The cauliflower will keep in the fridge for up to 3 months.

Note: *Nibble on this with a dish of yoghurt on the side to dip the florets into as you go.*

Jalapeños

I've included this lovely green and very common chilli throughout this book as an element in recipes. But this time they are the ferment.
   At the end of summer and all through autumn (fall) the market is full of different chillies, so don't hesitate to buy bulk to make hot sauces, add to brines, ferment in a simple brine solution and to have handy when you need to add zesty punch and flavour to another recipe. Fermented like this, they're not perfect to use with other vegetable ferments as they'll bring baggage (as in, almost start your ferment off – and maybe faster than you'd like). I prefer all of my ingredients to be about the same age when I put them in the jar, but for short ferments jalapeños are great, and work well as a kickstarter.

Preparation time: 15 minutes

Fermentation time: 2+ weeks
Equipment: 1 L (34 fl oz) jar, air-lock system

1 litre (34 fl oz/4 cups) water
2–3 tablespoons fine salt
about 500 g (1 lb 2 oz) fresh whole jalapeños or other chillies (or enough to fill your jar)
½ red onion, sliced
3–4 garlic cloves (or you could even use many more if you choose), peeled

Make a brine with the water and salt (page 66).
   Cram the jar full of the jalapeños, onion and garlic, then pour the brine over. Seal with your preferred air-lock system.
   Sit the jar in a nice, dark place for at least two weeks. Refrigerate when you decide it's ready, but it could sit on the bench for a while.

Garlic

I tend to ferment garlic in smaller jars, usually 500 ml (17 fl oz) in size, just so the peeling isn't too time consuming. Quite often, I'll peel a huge amount of garlic for my kimchi paste, and then grab a handful out to ferment like this or in honey (see page 200).

Preparation time: 10 minutes
Fermentation time: 5–10 days
Equipment: 500 ml (17 fl oz) jar, weight, air-lock system

500 ml (17 fl oz/2 cups) water (see notes)
2 teaspoons salt (see notes)
garlic cloves, peeled, enough to fill a jar three-quarters
pinch of oregano leaves or a sprig of tarragon (optional)

Make a brine with the water and salt (page 66).
 Pack the garlic into the jar, leaving enough room for a weight. A little oregano or tarragon is good in this ferment, so add some now if you like.
 Weigh the garlic down so it sits under the brine (see page 68). Seal the jar.
 The garlic cloves are ready within 5–10 days, or when the bubbling stops. Test them and keep on the counter for as long as you'd like, or refrigerate to keep indefinitely.

Notes: *The amount of water and salt will be different if you use a bigger or smaller jar (or more or less garlic). Aim for a 2% brine in this case.*
 Use this garlic in any of your cooking. It's particularly good in dressings, garlic butter or pesto, or pocketed into lamb or chicken before roasting.

Onions

I only really tried these onions quite recently, to be honest, because I grew up on pickled (vinegared) onions and loved them, and I was a bit worried wild fermentation would let me down. BUT it has come through again and these onions are sour and sweet and so good.

 I have used them on cheese platters and Danish open sandwiches, on top of tinned fish, and mixed in and on a burger. Do a big batch of onions like this and you'll soon find many ways to include them in your eating life. Then try the small pearl kind and have some whole ones for when you need to grab something out of the fridge. Eat an onion and a chunk of hard cheese with a glass of beer or wine. These onions will also break up raclette in a good way – always have fermented onions and pickles with raclette!

Preparation time: 10 minutes
Fermentation time: 5–10+ days
Equipment: 1 L (34 fl oz) jar, weight

1 litre (34 fl oz/4 cups) water
1 tablespoon salt
1 garlic clove, peeled
pinch of dried herbs, such as thyme, rosemary or tarragon
2 teaspoons mustard seeds
5–6 red, brown or white onions (enough to fill the jar three-quarters; see note), finely sliced

Make a brine with the water and salt (page 66).
 Pop the garlic, your choice of herb, and the mustard seeds into the bottom of the jar.
 Add the onion to the jar, making sure to leave room for the weight.
 Pour the brine over the onion. As usual, leave space between the top of the brine and the lid.
 Weigh down (see page 68), seal and sit out

of the light to ferment for 5–10 days, or until you like the taste, then refrigerate. The onions will keep in the fridge for months.

Note: *Another option is to use peeled whole baby onions instead of sliced large onions.*

Ginger

This is a great way of saving your ginger, of course, but also lovely with a curry or sushi. Young ginger works best. Consider buying big when ginger is in season and fermenting for later.

Preparation time: 15 minutes or 1 hour if making it pink (see notes)
Fermentation time: 1–4 weeks
Equipment: 1 L (34 fl oz) jar, weight

1 litre (34 fl oz/4 cups) water
about 1 tablespoon fine salt
3–4 large pieces of fresh ginger

Make a brine with the water and salt (page 66).

Scrub the ginger, then slice very finely with a mandoline (see notes). Pack it into the jar and pour the brine over, making sure to leave headroom. Add the weight and then seal. This ferment should take 1–4 weeks. Refrigerate it when ready and it will keep for 6 months.

Notes: *You could also leave the ginger whole and then slice it after fermenting. If you want pink, sushi-style ginger, add a few red shiso leaves and a tablespoon of sugar or mirin per 500 ml (17 fl oz/2 cups) water in the brine. Simmer for 20 minutes. Squeeze the leaves to get as much colour as possible, let the brine cool, then add the pink liquid to your ginger. See page 205 for a variation on this recipe.*

Turmeric

Everybody knows about the nutritional benefits of turmeric and how its bioavailability increases when you eat it with black pepper, right? Sometimes, fresh turmeric is hard to find, so buy up when you see it and enhance it like this, ready to use whenever you need it. It's super handy in 'golden milk' or any smoothies you make. Add it to everything for the happy reason that you have it in your fridge, available any time.

Preparation time: 15 minutes
Fermentation time: 5+ days
Equipment: 350 ml (12 fl oz) jar, air-lock system

250 g (9 oz) fresh turmeric, chopped
½ teaspoon ground black pepper
½ teaspoon ground cumin
pinch of fine salt
1 tablespoon raw honey
1 tablespoon water
1 tablespoon coconut oil

Process the turmeric into a paste with a masticating juicer or blender, then add the remaining ingredients to make a smooth paste. (You could also finely grate the turmeric, and then stir in the remaining ingredients.) Press into a jar, leaving a bit of headroom, of course.

Seal the jar (an air-lock is good), and let it sit on the bench for about 5 days, refrigerating when it smells strong and still clean, but a little sour. It will keep in the fridge for about a year.

MANDOLINES ARE SO HANDY FOR THINLY SLICING
FINGERS OF GINGER (AND OTHER THINGS)

Preserved lemons

There are many different recipes and styles for preserving lemons. We have great weather for growing lemon trees in Australia and the need to preserve them is real – who wants to buy lemons out of season when they were dripping from your neighbour's tree just a few months earlier? When choosing which ones to use, don't bother using thick-skinned, lightweight lemons. Preserve the heavy, thin-skinned ones for the best results.

Having fermented garlic and lemons on your shelf all through the year, always at hand for your regular cooking – even for adding to other ferments – is a great thing. And preserving lemons is so easy that I get the kids to do it for me.

Preparation time: 20 minutes
Fermentation time: 1+ months
Equipment: 2 L (68 fl oz) jar, weight

315 g (11 oz/1 cup) coarse salt
10 lemons (or enough to fill the jar – depending
    on their size, you may need more for juice),
    quartered
palmful of peppercorns
2 bay leaves
5 cardamom pods

In a bowl, massage the salt into the lemons quite roughly, squeezing juice out of the lemons as you go. Mix through the peppercorns, bay leaves and cardamom pods.

Transfer the lemons to the jar and push down, packing tightly. Pour any juice from the bowl over the lemons – you may need to squeeze some other lemons to get enough juice to cover the lemons well, although so far due to juicy lemons, I've never had to.

Add a weight (see page 68). (Lulu has used a small apple that fitted in the jar and pushed them under the brine using the lid – fit just right.)

Seal the jar and leave at room temperature for a day or two, turning to disperse the salt and juices. Leave to cure in a cool place for about a month.

They will keep for about 12 months.

THERE ARE SO MANY USES FOR PRESERVED LEMONS:

— mix a bit of preserved lemon with chopped garlic and parsley and olive oil – it's delicious on pasta, risotto, or over steak or fish

— use in a fennel ferment

— marinate some olives by finely slicing preserved lemon rind, then toss it with sliced garlic and parsley and pour the mixture over the olives

— add to a salsa verde

— eat them by themselves as an accompaniment to a cold beer

— use in a tagine, or chop and add to couscous.

Milk & dairy

When dealing with dairy, the best, most consistent results come from using the purest and freshest milk, so aim for that. When you buy milk from a shop always choose the bottles at the back, with the longest use-by date, because don't forget that even though you may not notice it, milk ages like any fresh produce. It's not perfect for three weeks and suddenly off the next day. Fresh vegetables wither visibly – you can see them become flaccid and change colour. The life inside your milk ages, but almost secretly – unless you are fermenting it.

Yoghurts won't mind if your milk is a bit older because heat is involved in producing them, but cheeses will. And milk kefir will separate a lot quicker when made from older milk. Which is actually fine, but just be aware of this and get to know milk and choose your ferment accordingly – nobody uses a flaccid carrot in a salad, but you might use it in a soup or stew for example. Start thinking of your milk in similar terms. Try to find out about the milk you are buying and avoid buying cheap, supermarket-brand milk that's a mixture of milk sourced from many different farms. Better to get milk from the one farm if you can.

Then there is the whole raw milk discussion. It's a very controversial topic that seems blown out of proportion when you remember how long we've been consuming milk in far less sanitary conditions. We've only had home refrigeration for about 100 years, yet we drank milk before that and have had a relationship with dairy of all kinds for thousands of years. Before refrigeration, milk was consumed fresh and the remainder heated and fermented, made into butter or cheeses and various types of yoghurt.

Ideally, you would be able to source raw milk from a farmer you know or can get to know, and ferment with that because natural fermentation generally kills off any harmful bacteria anyway – the lactic acids in kefir, for example, make the environment impossible for many of the dangerous pathogenic bacteria to survive in.

Dairy is an interesting topic at the moment. People are avoiding it for various dietary or animal welfare reasons and are buying or making nut, soy, oat and rice milks instead. You can certainly ferment with these milks, but the bacteria don't stick around or enjoy it as their full-time gig, so you'll still need a bit of mammal milk every third batch or so.

We've fermented all kinds of milk: camel, goat milk, as well as cow and sheep. I'd love to try using buffalo milk as I've been told it makes the only kind of ghee worthy of praise, and it must make a beautiful homemade yoghurt. I can't stop thinking about it. We may need to get a buffalo of our own.

Yoghurt ... 5 'wheys'

1. Yoghurt from chilli stems

An heirloom culture is a lovely thing. But there are ways to make yoghurt without yoghurt, so if that's you, no worries, we'll start there first, the place that I arrived at last. I had been in raptures about getting an heirloom culture. Varma (that's him on page 54) watched quietly, letting me go on about it for a few days until he mentioned that's not how they did it at home.

Varma started with us at The Fermentary on his fourth day in Australia ... and on his 600th day working with us, after watching me talk about my yoghurt cultures, he let me know quite casually that he does it another way (or more correctly, his aunty does).

It turns out that in Southern India it is a pretty regular thing to make yoghurt – or curd – using the stems of chillies. A bit of tamarind works too. (I was told that the whole tamarind pod was needed, but I didn't have that so I just used a dab from a jar I had and it worked!) I'd read something about this method in one of Sandor Katz's books, but mostly people wrote of it in an experimental tone. Here was someone telling me it was the best way.

This method is so easy it makes all other yoghurt recipes seem a bit superfluous. I'm not sure that we can even call it yoghurt, maybe it's just a curd? There is an ever so slight chilli flavour to the first batch, but it's hardly worth mentioning. In fact, my girls couldn't tell the difference in a taste test, except that the chilli yoghurt is less sour. The fact that it is milder may make it even better than some other yoghurts. And if the chilli is too strong, go ahead and use

that batch in a raita or a savoury soup, and start your next batch from it. I have recently found out that dried chickpeas are also a good inoculant, simply add a few instead of chilli stems.

I actually don't know the science of the chilli method. The reason you will want to make other yoghurts, from a friend's batch, for example, might be because of the microbial diversity found in the other kind. However, since I can't give you the breakdown, and if you don't already have an heirloom starter culture or good yoghurt in your local shop, or a milk kefir grain, then Varma and I give you this!

Even if you do have an heirloom starter maybe you'd just like to do this because it's fun. And you're curious.

Preparation time: 1 hour
Fermentation time: 3+ hours
Equipment: 2 × 500 ml (17 fl oz) jars

1 litre (34 fl oz/4 cups) milk
4–6 chilli stems (yes, just the stems, pop the rest into a ferment)

Heat the milk in a saucepan for 20–30 minutes at about 80°C (175°F). Let it cool to around 40°C (105°F).

Pour the milk into the jars, and add the chilli stems (2–3 per jar). Lid and pop into your incubator for 3–10 hours. (This can simply be your oven barely on, under 50°C/120°F.) I leave mine overnight. The chilli stems will float to the top, so just pull them out before refrigerating and storing. The yoghurt will keep covered in the fridge for a couple of weeks.

YOGHURT MADE FROM TAMARIND PODS GIVES IT A DELICIOUS TANG

2. Yoghurt from tamarind, too

This curd is very mild, almost pudding-like. We love its flavour, and the fact that I always have tamarind paste in my cupboard means that I can make it whenever I like. If you want to taste the tamarind, you can mix the paste in from the bottom of the jar you've made the yoghurt in once it is ready.

Preparation time: 1 hour
Fermentation time: 3 + hours
Equipment: 2 × 500 ml (17 fl oz) jars or 1 × 1 L (34 fl oz) jar

1 litre (34 fl oz/4 cups) milk
1 tamarind pod, with shell, broken into small pieces, or 1 teaspoon tamarind paste (the oil will sit on the top, and the paste will remain on the bottom, but the flavour is nice)

Heat the milk in a saucepan for 20–30 minutes at about 80°C (175°F). Let it cool to around 40°C (105°F).

Pour the milk into a couple of jars, or one big jar, and add the tamarind. Lid and pop into your incubator for 3–10 hours. (This can simply be your oven barely on, under 50°C/120°F.) I leave mine overnight. The tamarind pod will float to the top, so just pull it out before refrigerating and storing. This will keep covered in the fridge for a couple of weeks.

3. 'Back-slopping' – how to reproduce yourself

Naturally fermented yoghurt doesn't use a powdered starter, but instead uses just yoghurt. This is called 'back-slopping'. The term 'back-slopping' is not very pretty but I love to say it. It refers to the practice of using a little bit of something already good to start up another one to make it again, and again. It's used in fermenting a lot and in this instance, it's a bit of yoghurt as a starter for another batch.

You can back-slop using regular supermarket yoghurts, or buy starter cultures (made in a laboratory somewhere) to make your homemade yoghurts. But let me tell you: back-slopping from commercial yoghurt doesn't usually last more than five times because the bacteria isn't strong enough to survive. The same thing applies to yoghurt made with a powdered starter culture.

If we are celebrating the magical, we ideally wouldn't use laboratory-grown, but even more importantly, if we are making something from scratch we don't really want to add laboratory-grown anything to our list of ingredients.

Don't worry, you can get good heirloom yoghurt cultures quite easily. You can buy them online, get them through word of mouth fermenting groups, or from a good shop-bought yoghurt (a local, small-batch, tub-set yoghurt from wholefood shops or good supermarkets is a good bet). You can buy starter cultures from the supermarket complete with the incubator or system and pots to make it in, usually with a starter culture. But I prefer the free way, 'The Art of Making Do'.

With any back-slopping, even though you may think it kind and generous or a sure-fire way to success, do not over-slop! Hold back. Less is more when back-slopping. It's the 'chick breaking out of the egg without help story' – the struggle makes them stronger. Spoil it and it gets lazy. Or something like that.

Yoghurt swatches

If I were with you I might draw you closer, and tell you in one of those loud whispers, just for dramatics: 'Did you know you can soak a cloth in yoghurt, dry it out and save it for another time? Put it in a book or something until the day you want to reinvigorate it? That's how we still have old yoghurt cultures today! Did you know that?'

Swatches of linen dipped in your yoghurt and dried are a wonderful gift, and I sometimes include them as a gift to take home at workshops. Sounds fairytale-esque, but it has been done many times through history – and it's so sad that most of us don't know about it. This is just yoghurt, but it brings home to me how many other different things we need to learn to save, like seeds, and ... music, old languages, stories.

I have an heirloom starter – I got it from Sandor Katz who got it from someone at Yonah Schimmel's Knishery in Brooklyn. They had it because at that knishery they have been back-slopping for over 80 years. And that first strain was apparently brought with them on their immigration from Poland, on a piece of linen that had been soaked in yoghurt, dried, and then

ABOVE: MY YOGHURT SWATCH
RIGHT: PERFECT LITTLE POT OF YOGHURT

hidden to await better times, perhaps when routines in the kitchen become the norm again.

Sandor brought his home on a cloth just to see if it worked. Apparently he forgot all about it, and months later opened a book and found it, reinvigorated it in a glass of warm milk, made a small jar from it, kept making from it, and that's what I have now. Pretty amazing! (Mine started off a bit yeasty tasting, but really started to bloom beautifully after the third time around.)

Know this: yoghurt is a tinkering, relax-in-the-kitchen kind of thing. Yoghurt making requires some light attention and a bit of time cooking and cooling the milk, but the technique is simple and the fermenting time is fast, especially once you have done it a couple of times.

Whey too good?

You have to make your own yoghurt as soon as you find out that it tastes better, that it's very easy and satisfying, and that the strained yoghurt industry produces more by-product than it does product! The whey is not extracted using large hanging strainers, but with machines using centrifugal force that really pulls out more proteins and acids than it should. This is the reason you now see more whey protein powders and whey in everything, including baby food.

If you are producing a lot of whey, use it. Apparently it's not good for our water systems, so you're better off freezing it in cubes to add to smoothies, dips, soups, pancakes, breads, stocks and cooking liquids; soaking your grains and legumes in it; or using it as a starter for sodas (see page 145) and vegetables. It's also a great fertiliser, good to add to chicken and pig food, or other pet's food as well.

If you were stuck with canned food, which has no life in it at all, you can open up the can, put a dash of whey in there to sit overnight, and that can give the vegetables some life back.

Yoghurt-making equipment

Have your thermometer and chosen jars clean. For the yoghurt to set, you need an incubator that can hold your jars consistently at a temperature of 38–43°C (100–110°F) for around 4 hours. Don't let the temperature thing make it seem hard, it isn't. Driving to the shop to buy yoghurt is hard. Think of yoghurt making as another foraging adventure.

For your incubator, there are a plethora of ways to keep the jars warm:

— in an oven at its lowest temperature (easiest option and my favourite)

— with a hot water bottle in an esky (cooler)

— in a rice cooker or slow cooker

— in a dehydrator

— using a heat pad from brewing or even pet shops in an insulated box (we use an old bar fridge)

— in a foam box, half-filled with hot water and with a thermometer stuck in the lid – so you can keep an eye on the temperature.

You can get fancy yoghurt making sets, or temperature controlled incubators, which are great, but I love the oven most, followed by the dehydrator or the bar fridge with heat pad, and third (no power?): the esky (cooler) with the hot water bottle.

Oh and seriously, if you have one of those blenders that heats ingredients and holds a temperature, like a Thermomix, do use it – it's almost a tool made for yoghurt making! I probably make yoghurt (and get my kids to make it) twice as much now I have one. Use the same recipe, but with your blender: add the milk, set the temperature to 80°C (175°F) and the timer for 15–20 minutes or longer, then leave on a low speed. Allow the milk to cool to 37°C (100°F), add the yoghurt and mix by giving it a quick whiz. Set the blender to 37°C (100°F) on the lowest speed for about 10 minutes. Pour the milk into jars and incubate it for at least 4 hours, depending on how sour you like your yoghurt.

Preparation time: ↓1 hour
Fermentation time: 4–12 hours
Equipment: food-grade thermometer, incubator (see equipment text), jars for storing

1 litre (34 fl oz) milk (cow, sheep or goat)
2–3 tablespoons yoghurt – a good shop-bought one or, even better, someone else's homemade yoghurt

In a saucepan over medium heat, warm the milk to around 86°C (186°F). The longer you leave it at this temperature, the thicker it will get; about 20–30 minutes is good. Some people leave this step out. Go ahead and experiment, but I have found that heating the milk this first time around makes for thicker yoghurt.

Take the milk off the heat and cool to about 43°C (110°F) – you can pop it in a bowl of icy water, or into a bowl you've had in the freezer, and just stir with the thermometer in it. This might seem like a lot of work, but making yoghurt gives you a lovely pottering sciency feeling. You look like you're doing something very intimidating, but actually you're just waiting. The yoghurt makes itself.

When the milk has cooled to about 43°C (110°F), add the yoghurt and stir it in well. Maybe take a cup of milk out first and stir the yoghurt into that so you know it's properly mixed in.

You can now jar and lid it, and pop it into your incubator. The jar size doesn't really matter; you can simply use jam jars, or bigger 1 L (34 fl oz) jars.

Watch the temperature, letting it work until it is set to yoghurt – overnight, or after about 4 hours. Then put it in the fridge. It will get tangier the longer it sits after setting.

Yoghurt making complete! Consume within a couple of weeks. Maybe you'll dip some linen in your yoghurt to keep for your kids (see page 87).

Notes: *WAIT! THIS IS IMPORTANT. Always keep one jar hidden in the fridge for your next batch. Write on this jar 'Don't eat', or something similar. That's your starter for next time.*

Keep your yoghurt going, alive and ready to share the love. You'll have yoghurt you can give to your friends as a starter.

And something to consider: in the initial period where you heat the milk, adding flavours like cardamom, cinnamon or vanilla can be a lovely way to flavour yoghurt without adding sugar. Experiment! I particularly like cardamom – add a few pods in and strain before you put the yoghurt into the jars to incubate.

4. Kefir yoghurt

With yoghurt, the culture you use is important, but even more so is the process and technique. So back-slopping with some milk kefir (see page 102) also produces a beautiful yoghurt.

The directions are the same as with the yoghurt opposite, only the milk kefir is the starter. I use a little more milk kefir than yoghurt.

5. Vietnamese yoghurt

That's what we call it in our house because my daughter Bella had this when she was home-staying in Vietnam. This is the rough recipe from a 16-year-old's eyes and memory. We tried it and it's pretty delicious! It's certainly one that Lulu makes a lot now … because she's a sweet tooth, and because it's that easy.

Preparation time: 15 minutes
Fermentation time: 4+ hours
Equipment: food-grade thermometer, incubator (see equipment text on page 90), jars for storing

- 1 × 350 g (12½ oz) can sweetened condensed milk
- 2 × cans boiling water (can is used as measure)
- 1 × can room-temperature water (can is used as measure)
- ½ can plain, good yoghurt (can is used as measure)

Empty the can of condensed milk into a large bowl then add the three cans of water. (For a

AFTER I'VE EMPTIED THE CONDENSED MILK CAN, I USE IT AS THE MEASURE FOR THE OTHER INGREDIENTS

thicker, creamier yoghurt substitute 1 can of water for milk.)

When the mixture has cooled to about 40°C (105°F), add the yoghurt and mix very well.

Pour into jars and lid.

Incubate at around 45°C (113°F); see page 90.

The yoghurt will thicken within a few hours, getting sour as it goes. Try it after 4–5 hours. If it's sour enough, put it in the fridge. It will keep for a couple of weeks.

Notes: *If your condensed milk didn't come in a can, know that the ratio is 1 part condensed milk, 2 parts boiling water and 1 part room-temperature water (or milk) and ½ part yoghurt.*

Here's a fun thing! Because you are adding boiling water, you can flavour the water by steeping some cocoa nibs, chilli, cinnamon and a vanilla pod in it. Or try rose hip tea and then mix dried rose petals through the finished yoghurt. Or maybe get creative and use some earl grey tea and then lemon zest at the end.

The girls love this with a bit of nutmeg or cinnamon and chopped bananas. They put it in moulds in the freezer with shaved milk chocolate – stracciatella style. I like it because they make it themselves, and it's great when we don't have any fresh milk in the house. All kids seem to adore sweetened condensed milk. Fermentation means that the sugar gets eaten as it turns into yoghurt ... less sugar at least?

Buying sweetened condensed milk for the Vietnamese yoghurt sent me on a bit of a journey. When I was teaching in Japan 20 years ago, the men in the staffroom made 'pour-over'
coffee and sipped it pretty loudly. Years later in Melbourne that has become a thing, and I live with a man who prefers pour-over coffee. When I first sent the kids down to the shop to buy condensed milk for this yoghurt, I got them to buy me some instant coffee as well.

They bought one in a tin with 'gourmet' on it for my 'special coffee'. I felt nostalgic for the kind you get in some parts of Asia, you know, in a glass with the condensed milk down the bottom and the coffee sitting on top? Maybe it's a holiday association, but I really love that coffee. Shh. I'm pretty sure it's uncool in the coffee scene.

LOVING YOUR YOGHURTS & EATING THEM TOO — SOME IDEAS

Sometimes I end up with too much yoghurt, but need to keep making it to keep the culture strong. That's when I use it in drinks, frozen foods, soups, dips, cheeses and marinades. The soups are dear to my heart and a gorgeous way to enjoy yoghurt as part of a main meal in winter or summer.

QUICKIES

— Use yoghurt to replace sour cream in soups or mix it with sriracha to make a quick dip.

— Grab a smallish jar, pop some good jam or honey in the bottom, a bit of crunchy granola, fill it with yoghurt, lid it and take it to work. The girls make this for themselves for recess. Easy. When you add jams and honey to your own yoghurt, you'll notice a bit of water around it as the yoghurt enjoys the sugar. It's fine.

— To a bowl of yoghurt, add a good honey, some chopped peaches and some chopped nuts, such as almonds. (Shelled and chopped pistachios or almonds, topped with honey and yoghurt makes a beautiful breakfast. You run your spoon around the bottom, catching all the sweet, nutty and sour flavours on the way, for a perfect mouthful each time.)

— Blend yoghurt into a smoothie with a banana, some maple syrup and cinnamon, then decant it into popsicle moulds and freeze it.

AS A MARINADE

Yoghurt tenderises meat. When marinating, avoid using too much acid. The molecules start to toughen rather than tenderise. Spices tend to bloom in yoghurt, buttermilk and kefir, so it's the perfect way to imbibe flavours. Start with simply salt and yoghurt for fried chicken. Think tandoori and then move on to kimchi juice or chopped kimchi blended in yoghurt. Or a mix of spices. I lean towards chicken for this marinade, but it's certainly not limited to it. Marinate in the fridge anywhere from 30 minutes to overnight, or even a couple of days.

AS A DRESSING

Any of the following dressings can be used to top a sliced cos (romaine) or iceberg lettuce, or slathered on a plate as a base for a salad, drizzled over a grilled vegetable platter, or spooned onto roasted vegetables. Honey (or better still, Fermented honey & garlic, page 200) poured over whole small carrots and roasted for 45 minutes works particularly well with the Yoghurt with tahini dressing (page 96).

Yoghurt 'caesar' dressing

4 garlic cloves, crushed
4 tablespoons yoghurt
1 tablespoon mustard (your own, I hope)
2 teaspoons red wine vinegar or
   kombucha vinegar
5 anchovies, chopped
about 2 tablespoons lemon juice
125 ml (4 fl oz/½ cup) olive oil
salt and pepper, to taste

Add all the ingredients except the olive oil and salt and pepper to a blender. Pulse until blended, then slowly add the oil in a steady stream. Taste, and season with salt and pepper.

THE BEST KIND OF TAKE-AWAY SWEET
TREAT: HONEY, NUTS & YOGHURT

This will keep in the fridge for a few days. It may need a good shake or stir before use.

Notes: To make your own mustard, see page 202. This dressing is ideal for a caesar salad, but don't limit yourself to that.

Creamy dill dressing

250 g (9 oz/1 cup) yoghurt
1–2 spring onions (scallions), finely chopped
2 tablespoons lemon or lime juice
1 tablespoon apple cider vinegar
1–2 garlic cloves, crushed
60 ml (2 fl oz/¼ cup) olive oil
½ teaspoon fresh or dried dill
salt and pepper, to taste

Whisk all the ingredients to combine. This dressing will keep in the fridge for a few days.

Yoghurt with tahini dressing

250 g (9 oz/1 cup) yoghurt
2 tablespoons tahini
1 garlic clove, crushed
salt and pepper, to taste
squeeze of lime
dash of sriracha sauce or kimchi juice, to taste

Mix all the ingredients together in a bowl. Transfer to a jar and it will keep in the fridge for at least a week. Shake well before using.

Note: For a sweeter dressing include some honey and omit the garlic, or use the Fermented honey & garlic (page 200).

AS A DIP

Of course yoghurt is a good savoury dip. If you find your yoghurt a bit runny, strain it in some muslin (cheesecloth) for an hour or so first.

Tzatziki

1 cucumber, grated
375 g (13 oz/1½ cups) yoghurt
2 garlic cloves, peeled and finely chopped
½ teaspoon salt
2 tablespoons olive oil
handful of chopped mint
1 teaspoon finely chopped dill leaves

This dip is best when you have time to drain the grated cucumber in muslin overnight. If you are that organised, you should also mix the yoghurt with the garlic, salt and oil and let it sit in the fridge overnight. The next day, mix the yoghurt with the drained cucumber, mint and dill. This will keep in the fridge for about a week.

Note: This dip is great with pitta chips, on lamb, or as a dip for anything. We always serve it with Roger's chilli chicken (page 64). Roger prefers to cut the cucumber into small cubes after seeding it and peeling it, and adds a handful of coriander (cilantro) leaves as well. Probably better? He's the chef, after all.

Carrot raita

2–3 carrots, peeled and grated
1 teaspoon ground cumin, plus an extra pinch
500 g (1 lb 2 oz/2 cups) yoghurt
1 teaspoon salt
2 green chillies, finely chopped
ghee or oil, for frying
1 teaspoon mustard seeds
½ cup coriander (cilantro) leaves

Pour boiling water over the carrot and let sit for about 10 minutes. Drain, then squeeze the moisture out. Combine the carrot with the cumin, yoghurt, salt and some of the chilli.

In a frying pan, heat some ghee and add the mustard seeds. Cook them until they pop (making sure they don't burn), then add the remaining chilli and an extra pinch of cumin. Combine this mixture with the yoghurt mixture and garnish with the coriander leaves. It will keep in the fridge for about a week.

Note: Serve this dip with warm bread. It's a good one to put in a lunchbox with pitta bread.

Spinach dip

500 g (1 lb 2 oz) spinach, washed and finely chopped
500 g (1 lb 2 oz/2 cups) yoghurt
1–2 garlic cloves, crushed
salt and pepper, to taste
2 tablespoons walnuts, roughly chopped

Put the spinach in a frying pan over medium heat, with a splash of water, and add the lid to steam it until soft. Drain, cool, squeeze the moisture out, then combine it in a bowl with the yoghurt, garlic and salt and pepper. Sprinkle the walnuts on top when serving.

The dip will keep in the fridge for a few days, but may need a stir.

Note: If you want to be '80s, serve the dip in a bread bowl ... I like being '80s. Hollow out a medium-sized round bread loaf and pop it into a warm (180°C/350°F) oven to crisp up. Fill it with the spinach dip (walnuts mixed through). You could sprinkle grated cheddar over the top and stick it back into the oven until the cheese has melted and the dip is warm. Sit around the loaf, pull bits of bread off and dip them in.

TO FERMENT WITH

Chillies in yoghurt

Yoghurt is living, so can naturally be used to impart its life to preserve other things. Or maybe it's the salt doing that? I came across this recipe and tried it because we have so much yoghurt sometimes. It's the opposite of the chilli stems making yoghurt: this is the yoghurt preserving the chillies.

1 bunch of long, plump chillies
yoghurt (enough to cover the chillies)
oil, for deep-frying

Slice the chillies carefully, keeping them intact at the top and the tail. Pop them into a shallow dish and cover with the yoghurt, then a towel. Leave on your bench for about 5 days, then pop into your dehydrator on 41°C (106°F). (If you don't have a dehydrator, dry in the oven overnight at the lowest possible temperature – below 50°C/122°F.) Dehydrate, with the yoghurt still on them, until dry, then keep in an airtight container. (The real way would be to sit them out in the sun, but I'm in Melbourne and the sun is unpredictable.)

To serve, you need to deep-fry them.

Note: These are a really beautiful snack with a glass of beer or kombucha.

Overnight yoghurt rice

This is something I've stumbled across lately through Varma. I make this with our rice cooker on the warm setting overnight, but if you don't have one you could do it in the pan you cooked your preferred rice in and keep it in a very low oven overnight.

While your pot of cooked rice is still warm, add a couple of tablespoons of yoghurt and some milk, not enough to make it soupy, but just enough that it will be soaked up overnight. Ferment in the rice cooker on low, or in the pan in a very low oven. As it ferments, the starch in the rice is eaten and the yoghurt penetrates the rice, changing the texture somewhat.

Note: *Try it for breakfast with a sprinkle of nutmeg and maple syrup, or add some to a jar with fresh mango, coconut and some seeds, lid it up and pack it for school or wherever you go during the day.*

IN A SOUP

Hearty Persian yoghurt soup (*Ash-e mast* or *Yayla çorbasi*)

This soup is fresh and completely nourishing. It has a soul-soothing, heartwarming quality that makes you long for more. I had wanted this recipe after having it at a friend's house in Belgium, and then here in Melbourne a colleague gave it to me after she heard I was writing this book! Meryem has very fond memories of rolling the meatballs with her late great-grandmother. It is a nice thing to do with children – they love to roll the balls and chat, and you can keep them busy doing that while you get the rest ready. Just know that there will be some yellow hands afterwards.

I love the mixture of textures – it reminds me of a Greek lemon and rice soup. Make sure to really mince the onion so it doesn't stick out and fall from the little meatballs as you roll and cook them. If you don't think you can chop the onion finely enough, cook it with the turmeric and ghee, let it cool, then mix through with the meat. If you use beef broth, a really good one does make a difference – make it the day before when you soak the chickpeas.

SERVES: 6–8

110 g (4 oz/½ cup) dried chickpeas, rinsed and soaked overnight, rinsed again and drained, or 400 g (14 oz) tinned chickpeas, drained
1.5 litres (51 fl oz/6 cups) water (or even better, beef broth)
100 g (3½ oz/½ cup) white rice
about ½ cup dill and chives, chopped
1 egg yolk, or 1 teaspoon cornflour (cornstarch)
250 g (9 oz/1 cup) yoghurt, at room temperature
salt and pepper, to taste

MEATBALLS
2–4 tablespoons ghee, or a combination of
    butter and oil
1 teaspoon ground turmeric, or 1.5 cm (½ in)
    piece of turmeric, freshly ground
salt and pepper, to taste
1 onion, finely chopped
250 g (9 oz) minced (ground) beef or lamb

TOPPING
1 large onion, finely sliced
4 garlic cloves, chopped
2 tablespoons ghee
½ cup chopped fresh mint

Put the chickpeas in a large stockpot, cover
with the water, and bring to a boil. Lower the
heat and cook until the chickpeas are tender,
between 45 minutes and 1½ hours. (Or if using
tinned chickpeas, cover with the same amount
of water, heat, add the rice and simmer for
20 minutes, adding water if it gets too low.)

To make the meatballs, melt the ghee and
cook the turmeric, salt and pepper for a few
minutes. Take off the heat, let cool somewhat,
then mix through the onion and beef. Roll into
tiny balls (the size you'd want in your soup).

When the chickpeas are tender, add the rice
and cook for a further 20 minutes, adding water
if it gets too low (unless you've already done
this step, using tinned chickpeas). Add the dill
and chives, stir, then gently slide in the little
meatballs. Cook for a further 20 minutes.

Whisk the egg yolk (or cornflour) with three
teaspoons of the yoghurt. Blend the mixture
with the rest of the yoghurt and add it to the
soup. Cook on low heat until heated through,
then season with salt and pepper, to taste.

Make the topping by frying the onion and
garlic in the ghee until golden. Add the mint and
sauté for a few more minutes. Garnish the soup
with the topping, and serve.

Ferment for good
Milk & dairy

IN A DRINK

Ayran or doogh

There are many versions of this drink around
Turkey and Iran. It's a refreshing Persian
drink similar to a lassi, but thinner and not as
sweet, and maybe more refreshing. There must
be recipes similar to this all over the place,
particularly in regions where it gets really hot.
It reminds me of the Japanese drink 'Calpis',
which is made commercially with lactic acid,
water and milk powder. It's roughly based on the
flavour of the ancient Mongolian drink *kumis*,
which was originally made from mare's milk – a
lot sweeter than cow's apparently. Some people
add a carbonated water instead of plain, but if
you leave it on your bench for a day it should get
pretty carbonated. As usual, make sure to keep
an eye on it and refrigerate before drinking.

SERVES: 4–6

250 g (9 oz/1 cup) yoghurt
750 ml (25½ fl oz/3 cups) water
7–8 fresh or dried mint leaves
salt, to taste

Mix all the ingredients in a jug and cover loosely.
Sit it on your bench for a while, anywhere
from an hour to a day or two, making sure to
leave headroom, as a bit of air is important.
Refrigerate before drinking.

Note: Phudina chaas, *another version, has
1 teaspoon of roasted cumin and a tiny amount
of ground green chilli added. Add the spices
with the salt to the recipe above.*

Salty lassi

The body needs salt in a hot climate, and I think a salty yoghurt drink is more delicious than the sweet kind. My kids don't agree though! They go for a mango lassi any day.

SERVES: 4–6

1 teaspoon cumin seeds
handful of ice cubes
250 ml (8½ fl oz/1 cup) water
1 or 2 pinches of salt, to taste
600 g (1 lb 5 oz) yoghurt

Toast the cumin in a dry frying pan over medium heat and then grind. Add it and the remaining ingredients to a blender and blitz until smooth.

Note: *Omit the cumin and use less ice if you like.*

Sweet mango lassi

You could use any fruit for this, but mango is most popular in our house. Some people add a sweetener; do that if you like, but I prefer not to. I often buy mangoes when they are cheap and peel, seed and freeze them. This means no need to use ice cubes or as much water.

SERVES: 4–6

500 g (1 lb 2 oz/2 cups) yoghurt
1 mango, peeled, seed removed
handful of ice cubes
pinch of salt
500 ml (17 fl oz/2 cups) water

Pop all the ingredients into a blender and blitz until smooth. Serve in glasses and drink at any time of the day, even for breakfast. So refreshing and healthy.

Sweet Punjabi lassi

SERVES: 4–6

500 g (1 lb 2 oz/2 cups) yoghurt
about 375 ml (12½ fl oz/1½ cups) water or milk
1–2 dates, or 75 g (2¾ oz/⅓ cup) sugar or
    coconut syrup, honey or maple syrup
6–8 ice cubes
a few threads of saffron, to serve
1 teaspoon ground cardamom, to serve

Blitz all the ingredients except the saffron and cardamom in a blender. You may choose to add less water if you are after a thicker consistency.

Sprinkle some saffron and ground cardamom on top when serving, to make it look fancy.

Note: *If you like rosewater, add 2 teaspoons.*

CHILLIES IN YOGHURT (PAGE 97)

Milk kefir

Kefir actually translates to 'pleasure' or 'feeling good', and for good reason – it is my chosen powerhouse ferment to heal almost anything.

In order to make milk kefir, you first need to get hold of a SCOBY (symbiotic colony of bacteria and yeast). Milk kefir SCOBYs are known as 'grains' purely because of their shape, but are in fact a polysaccharide matrix of bacteria and yeast. With one little grain, you hold the power to ferment milk, make yoghurt, labneh and a myriad of cheeses, including hard, soft and blue.

This book won't provide you with recipes for cheesemaking. I don't want to smother your enthusiasm with too many steps, so go ahead and get confident with the recipes I've given you first, then 'level up' to cheeses. In the meantime use your imagination with kefir – it has yeasts and so can be used for so many purposes. With just these magical, exuberant, living kefir grains you can raise simple breads and pancakes, and make yoghurt, labneh, crème fraîche, milk kefir, cultured butter, smoothies, ice creams and dressings. Anything buttermilk can do, milk kefir can do better. The list of possibilities really only stops where your patience or imagination (or tolerance for some failure) does.

In ordinary kitchen life – even an avid fermenter's ordinary kitchen life – you may not want a fridgeful of different cultures, nor a benchful. Really, if I had to choose one SCOBY (and I hate to say it because I love all of them) milk kefir is the one.

Milk kefir is simply fermented milk, similar to drinking yoghurt. Just like any of the other yeasts and bacteria (and us!) the SCOBYs are attracted to sugars, and in the case of milk, the lactose.

Speaking of lactose ... don't miss out on milk kefir because you don't normally consume cow's milk. Kefir is more digestible than unfermented milk, is a rich source of protein, calcium and B vitamins, and has many more strains of bacteria than any yoghurt. The many strains of lactobacillus in the milk kefir eat the lactose in the milk, turning it into lactic acids, which are what gives kefir its lovely, sour, yoghurty taste.

Milk kefir is a gypsy's dream. Once you're addicted and comfortable with it, you'll probably take it with you on holidays, work trips, camping, weekend sojourns – not only because it's delicious, but also because it is mesophilic, meaning it ferments at room temperature – no need for an incubator. All you require is milk and a jar, and the next day you've got your regular source of goodness. Pack your tablespoon of grains into a zip-lock bag, store the package in the jar you plan on pouring the milk into and there you have it. There's no need to even dehydrate the grains. The other SCOBYs need more ingredients, aren't quite as practical to transport, take longer to ferment and require other bottles, etc. Not milk kefir.

If you are travelling, you can even pop your milk kefir SCOBY into juices now and then and treat them a bit like water kefir for a sweet, delicious bubbly drink. Just remember that they prefer milk from goats, sheep, cows and camels (and probably buffalo too, but I've never tried this) over juice or other milks. So take care of their needs and don't push them too far.

Most commercially produced milk kefirs are made with powders that mimic the real thing and are usually pasteurised. It's quite hard to create the real thing on a commercial scale, so making your own is almost the only way you're going to get authentic kefir. There are a couple of companies producing and selling traditionally made milk kefir (ours for one), so check your area for what is available. The powdered form of kefir you buy from the health food shop will only last three to five rotations before you need to buy more, which is the opposite to real kefir – it grows so that you have it for a lifetime.

WHERE DID THE FIRST KEFIR GRAIN COME FROM?

One possibility is that it formed from the stomach-skin bag used by goat herders. Mongolians have something very similar to milk kefir, made from mare's milk in bags that are jiggled every time someone walks through the room, or hung on a horse as they travel. But no one can actually make a milk kefir grain from scratch; really it is no more possible to make an apple seed than a milk kefir grain. We can mimic the strains that are found in milk kefir but we can't make the grain.

There are a few folklorish stories surrounding milk kefir's history. Kefir cheese was recently discovered in a tomb of a Chinese mummy. However, according to Islamic legend, the Prophet Muhammad gifted some kefir grains to the people of the Caucasus Mountains who guarded them with their life, calling them 'The Grains of the Prophet'. They believed their potency might weaken if they shared them around, so they kept the method of making milk kefir secret. Marco Polo even writes of kefir on his eastern travels.

In the 20th century, Russian doctors knew about the health-giving milk kefir and wanted to produce enough for everyone in the hospital system. (Impressive, forward thinking, right? How wonderful it would be if we could get real foods like this in our hospitals!) They approached a dairy owned by two brothers to search some out; they in turn sent a gorgeous employee, Irina Sakharova, to coax some from a prince called Bek-Mirza, who denied it to her. He had her kidnapped and tried to marry her, but she held off and in the end, was let go and as an apology, was given four and a half kilograms (10 lb) of milk kefir grains. Apparently Irina was given an award by the Russian government when she was 95 years old (or something like that). There's even a statue of a lady with a cup of kefir welcoming people to the town of Karachayevsk. Dedicated.

My loyal customer Sandy loves our kefir, especially the milk version. She was an early adopter – a fan from long ago when we were still working out of a shed at the winery. Her dog was quite ill and I mentioned that feeding him a milk kefir grain or two, or even a little milk kefir with his food, might make him feel better. She did this and his demeanour and vitality changed immensely. He still had cancer, but the effects of feeding him milk kefir changed the way he got around, and reduced inflammation to the point that everyone was remarking on it, including her vet. She became an avid convert – and a great supporter, drinking it herself and telling everyone she knew about it.

Sandy has a bed and breakfast in country Victoria, and wanted me to flavour the milk kefir for her. I was doing a gorgeous black sesame paste, vanilla and coconut sugar version at the time, as well as a maple, vanilla and cinnamon combo – just for a few people. It's not a great thing to sell commercially because the sugar feeds the bacteria and yeasts, and when you add that much and seal the bottle the fizz can get very powerful. Sandy called one Sunday, saying she just couldn't open the bottle. It was

making violent fizzy sounds – and there was no way she could open it. No amount of waiting helped. Uh oh. I told her to go outside to the compost area and point it towards the ground and open it there. She hung up. Instead, she put two plastic bags over the top and opened it slowly, trying to release and burp the gases as she went, but alas, the cap shot off! Milk kefir spurted out so powerfully that it burst through the two bags and up onto her ceiling and down onto every little thing in her kitchen. Oops. That's the moral of the story: when you flavour the milk kefir and put it back in the fridge it keeps, but don't make it too sweet, or leave it out too long.

Milk kefir

Using the freshest milk possible is important here, however your milk kefir will still ferment with older milk.

Be sure to give your jar a wash and good dry beforehand, but don't be too caught up in making a very sterile environment.

Preparation time: 5 minutes
Fermentation time: 24–48 hours
Equipment: 1 × 500 ml (17 fl oz) glass jar, muslin (cheesecloth) or lid, bottle for storing

500 ml (17 fl oz/2 cups) milk (you could also use coconut milk, almond milk or soy milk – see notes)
about 50 g (1¾ oz) milk kefir grains

Put the milk and the kefir grains into the jar, cover with a lid or muslin secured with a rubber band, and let it sit for 12–24 hours at normal room temperature. (Some people lid their kefir, and others use a cloth – if you do use a cloth,

keep it away from other aerobic ferments such as kombucha or any other yeasts, as they can be bad for it.)

If you experience a little separation don't worry – maybe you've over-fermented, or maybe the milk wasn't as fresh as it could have been. It's still fine. Just mix after you strain it.

Strain with a fine strainer (see notes), bottle and refrigerate the liquid. It should be thicker than milk, but still pourable, and smell lovely, fresh and sour, like Greek-style yoghurt. It will probably be slightly fizzy; that's my favourite part! If not, set it out for a further night on your bench and give it a gentle shake. The longer it sits out to ferment, the more lactose is eaten and the sourer and fizzier it will become.

Notes: *You can also ferment using coconut milk, almond or soy milk. Milk kefir grains definitely prefer cow's or goat's milk so, if you use these other plant milks, make sure to rest the grains with a good feed of real milk every couple of ferments.*

You can easily make kefir part of your routine. Find out how much you'll drink and only make as much as that, as the grains prefer to remain in use rather than being used in large batches and put to rest. The grains should grow and can get quite big. They can also be 'put to sleep' in the fridge covered with a little milk in a jar should you need a break, or can be frozen or even dehydrated at under 40°C (104°F) to save for another time. Excess milk kefir grains can be blended into smoothies or fed to animals.

There are plenty of rumours about never using steel sieves or metal of any kind. I've always used a metal strainer, and we even ferment the milk kefir in high-grade stainless steel at The Fermentary. Plastic is okay too, but don't go out and buy new plastic stuff. Metal things from your cupboard are fine.

MILK KEFIR GRAIN

After you've bottled the kefir and it's in your fridge, whey and kefir layers may occur, either at the top or the bottom. It's fine to mix it all in together when you drink it, or tip the whey out to use in a ferment as a starter or in a juice for the protein. If you are getting whey separation and really thick fermented kefir rising to the top of the bottle during fermentation, then your milk is either tainted or old, or maybe your grains are out of balance. It may be a good idea to tip that batch out and start again.

There is a tangy, effervescent, deep, almost goaty flavour to milk kefir that you'll grow to love – like a drinkable feta cheese. How sour it gets will depend on how long you ferment it for. I like a good 48 hours, but many prefer 24 hours. I've found that in the warmer weather, covering it with muslin (cheesecloth) is probably better, as it ferments more slowly and more gently, resulting in a lower alcohol content.

Second ferment:

Generally with milk kefir, as soon as it's fermented you would pop it into the fridge. But if your aim is for less lactose and for a fizz, you can leave it out for a further 12–24 hours. During this time you could also add some flavours, as you would for a second ferment in kombucha or water kefir. Experiment with this if you like. I've found these combinations work well:

— macha powder and coconut sugar

— dash of coffee or some coffee beans

— cinnamon stick and vanilla pod or drop of vanilla (you can re-use this)

— a couple of cardamom pods or a pinch of ground cardamom with ground pistachios.

LOVING YOUR MILK KEFIR & USING IT TOO — SOME IDEAS

Milk kefir is a versatile, delicious, healthy addition to smoothies and juices, and can be poured over granolas and frozen into popsicles. You can very easily make a yummy smoothie by popping any frozen fruit and some kefir into a blender and blitzing. You can also freeze your kefir into large ice cubes and add them to your smoothies like that. Kefir freezes well and the beneficial bacteria survive … so freeze away!

STIR-IN SMOOTHIES

The below ideas are great because you can just stir them into a glass with no need for a blender. Or if you're making a bottleful, just add flavours straight into the bottle or jar and shake to mix.

Use your favourite sweetener; I generally use maple or coconut syrup as a sweetener. These combinations are favourites here at home and at the markets – quantities of each are up to you.

— maple syrup, ground cinnamon and vanilla extract

— honey and ground cinnamon (ground cardamom is good too)

— dash of cooled brewed coffee and raw sugar

— chai tea – brew some strong and add to your milk kefir with a sweetener if needed

— black sesame paste, coconut sugar and vanilla extract

— your favourite jam or marmalade – or even lemon butter

— apple (or other fruit) syrup and cinnamon

— ground turmeric, cinnamon, ginger, black pepper and coconut sugar.

BLACK SESAME, COCONUT SUGAR &
VANILLA MILK KEFIR SMOOTHIE

BLENDER SMOOTHIES

It's nice to have an array of frozen fruit on hand to make kefir smoothies nice and thick and cold. Also consider popping in any sweet leftover cooked vegetables or fruits, such as sweet potato, carrots or even apple sauce. I haven't given quantities here because I don't want to be pedantic – you should taste as you go. Generally, for 1 litre (34 fl oz/4 cups) of milk kefir, 1 banana is plenty, and a handful of berries is good too.

Adding milk kefir to any smoothie will help retain its colour, and of course adds all the probiotics you need. It's best to add the fruit, frozen or harder foods first and give it a whiz, adding your liquids and blending until smooth. Try these flavour ideas:

— berries (blueberries, raspberries, blackberries are all delicious), maple syrup and vanilla

BERRY MILK KEFIR SMOOTHIE

— banana, cinnamon, vanilla and maple syrup

— peaches and vanilla

— mango

— cacao or chocolate and ground cinnamon

— almond butter and ground cinnamon

— nut butter and jam

— avocado, macha and honey

— pear, cocoa and vanilla

— lychee, cocoa and ginger juice

— ground ginger, nutmeg and cinnamon, cooked sweet potato, maple syrup and walnuts or nut butter

— ground ginger, medjool dates and honey

— any 'super greens' with a sweetener.

YOU DON'T HAVE TO FLAVOUR MILK KEFIR
AT ALL. ROGER PREFERS IT PLAIN

A BIT OF KEFIR ADVICE

— It's great to have a glass first thing in the morning as it relaxes a nervous tummy; it also seems to work like a mild appetite suppressant. I am a person who thinks of eating a lot, but when I first started to drink kefir every morning in a smoothie, I didn't think about eating until lunchtime, which is impressive for me.

— A shot before bed is also good – apparently milk kefir contains tryptophan (among many other amazing things), which is a relaxant. Milk kefir goes in and lines your gut, allowing all of the bacteria to settle in and do their thing, which is great for people with gut issues. Roger drinks almost a bottle of this a day and it has healed his reflux.

— Pour leftover smoothies into popsicle moulds and freeze for a healthy snack that feels like a treat. They're great for when kids are a bit sick and need some probiotics and easy nutrients put into their tummies.

— Use milk kefir instead of milk in your ice-cream maker with any of the smoothie flavours for a delicious frozen yoghurt.

— Use milk kefir to replace buttermilk in any recipe – it makes great pancakes, is good for soaking bircher muesli, and can be used as the rising agent in breads.

— Your sourdough will go crazy if you add some milk kefir to it.

— Pour over muesli or granola as is, or in smoothie form – even green smoothie form.

— If you love working with milk kefir, go a step further and look into making cheeses and even ice cream with it. It's easy to slip into a love affair with this one.

NOW THAT YOU HAVE MILK KEFIR YOU CAN MAKE:

Labneh

Eating labneh is a gorgeous way of getting your probiotics, and it couldn't be easier. If you can pour from a jar, then you can make labneh. It is particularly delicious when you use goat's or sheep's milk kefir, and is also a great kids' project – like most recipes here. You can also make labneh with yoghurt. You'll only get a bit of whey, but if you make it often, don't pour your whey down the sink – use it.

Labneh is best made with a thick kefir, so if it's still very thin, ferment it for a day or two longer, or use a double layer of muslin (cheesecloth) to hold it. While yoghurt might seem easier to turn into labneh because it's thicker, a good thick milk kefir is more flavourful and really does make the most delicious labneh.

1 litre (34 fl oz/4 cups) milk kefir (or 500 g/
    1 lb 2 oz/2 cups yoghurt)
1 teaspoon salt (optional)

FOR STORAGE IN OIL
1 teaspoon salt flakes
1 teaspoon black peppercorns
rosemary sprig
1 small chilli
1 garlic clove
good-quality olive oil

Line a strainer with some muslin, folded over a couple of times to make it very finely woven. Put the strainer into a bowl and pour the milk kefir onto the cloth. Wrap the cloth over itself and let sit on your bench for about 12–24 hours.

When it feels solid enough, add a teaspoon of salt (you can skip this part if you like). Tie the ends of the cloth together and tie it to something like a wooden spoon that can be hung over a bowl or sink. Resting it over a large saucepan is a good idea too. Give it a gentle squeeze to get any last juices out.

You'll need to judge when it's ready, but a day of hanging should be enough.

You can put this labneh into a jar as is, and eat it like cream cheese, or roll into small balls to store in a jar of oil. (It lasts longer this way.)

If you are going to store the labneh in oil, roll it into walnut-sized balls and arrange on a tray or chopping board lined with baking paper or a latex drying sheet. Refrigerate for a few hours or overnight to help them hold their shape.

Place the balls in a clean jar. Add the salt, peppercorns, rosemary, chilli and garlic (or other flavourings – see below for suggestions).

Slowly pour the olive oil over the balls. Make sure there are no air pockets left in there, then seal the jar and refrigerate. It will keep for more than a month if you don't eat it all first. A jar of labneh can disappear from our lunch or breakfast table in one sitting.

FLAVOURED LABNEH

You don't have to stick to the suggested ideas. There are no limits. Here are some additional flavour combinations:

— olive oil, few basil or parsley sprigs, 1 sun-dried tomato, 1 garlic clove, peppercorns and salt

— olive oil, sesame oil, 1 chilli, 1 teaspoon black pepper, preserved or fresh lemon zest and salt

— olive oil, lemon zest, pinch of saffron, pinch of ground cardamom and salt

Instead of storing in oil you could also make one or two larger balls and roll them in a flavoursome mixture. Here are some ideas:

— chopped fresh herbs, such as basil, parsley and mint with salt, to taste

— black and white sesame seeds, pinch of dulse flakes with salt, to taste

— crushed hazelnuts, with pinches of vanilla powder, ground cinnamon and coconut sugar – drizzle some maple syrup over the top and serve with fruit toast.

Or, spread labneh onto toast, a bagel or a cracker and top with some kraut, plop onto a sweet potato, dollop next to a slice of apple pie, on a wrap with tabouli, or onto smoked salmon on rye. You could also grate, salt and strain cucumbers and mix them through this labneh like a tzatziki, or even stir through some hot sauce as a dip.

Crème fraîche

Begin with a pourable cream – if you have a very thick cream (of the freshest and best quality) you can make it more pourable by adding and mixing through some milk. Australia tends to have very thick cream compared to the US.

Preparation time: 5 minutes
Fermentation time: 24+ hours
Equipment: 1 × 250 ml (8½ fl oz) jar or 1 × 1 L (34 fl oz) jar, muslin (cheesecloth)

TO MAKE A 250 ML (8½ FL OZ) JAR
1 decent-sized milk kefir grain
250 ml (8½ fl oz/1 cup) pouring (single/light) cream

TO MAKE A 1 L (34 FL OZ) JAR
1 generous tablespoon milk kefir grains
1 litre (34 fl oz/4 cups) pouring (single/light) cream

In the jar, combine the kefir grain/s and the cream, leaving some headroom. Cover with muslin and secure with a rubber band. Leave on the kitchen bench for about 24 hours, or perhaps longer depending on your taste, or the kefir and cream interaction.

Strain when it's lovely and sour. It may be too thick to strain, so you might have to fish around for the kefir grains. Put a lid on the jar and refrigerate. It works every time, but even so I still feel amazed and grateful. It will keep in the fridge for weeks.

Note: *I take out a small amount of crème fraîche and then turn the rest into butter (see below). That's why you should always try and make a 1 litre (34 fl oz) jar of it.*

Kefir cultured butter

This is an amazing butter. I think once you make a good one you'll think about it so much that you'll have to make it all the time. Don't worry about fishing the kefir grains out of the crème fraîche, because they'll pretty much pop out of the butter willingly.

MAKES: 1 PAD OF BUTTER

Equipment: 1 large jar

about 750 g (1 lb 11 oz/3 cups) kefir Crème fraîche (page 113)
iced water (plus more iced water ready to use while you are squeezing and massaging the butter)
salt, to taste (see note)

Place the crème fraîche into the jar – it should be about half to two-thirds full. Put the lid on and shake like crazy. It won't take that long – maybe a couple of minutes at most. The butter fat will separate from the whey pretty quickly.

Strain, and holding it in your hands, immerse the butter in icy water and squeeze it very gently to remove the whey. You don't want it melting all over your hands, so keep your hands cold by dipping them into some separate iced water.

Shape it and, most importantly (I think), salt it well with some beautiful salt. Cover and store in the fridge.

Note: *Experiment with different salts, or by adding other flavours – finely chopped black garlic, or anchovies, for example.*

Gözleme – savoury stuffed (kefir) bread

This is a filled and fried bread. There is a lot of good gözleme available in Melbourne, but not so much out in the country, so we have developed this kefir one.

SERVES: 4–6

sunflower oil, for frying
lemon wedges, to serve
250 g (9 oz/1 cup) yoghurt, to serve (optional)

KEFIR DOUGH
250 ml (8½ fl oz/1 cup) milk kefir
½ teaspoon soft butter (or sunflower oil)
pinch of salt
2 teaspoons sugar
300 g (10½ oz/2 cups) plain (all-purpose) flour
pinch of bicarbonate of soda (baking soda)

FILLING
2 tablespoons sunflower oil
4 spring onions (scallions), chopped
60 g (2 oz) spinach, chopped
2 tablespoons chopped dill
375 g (13 oz) Labneh (page 111) or feta, crumbled

To make the dough, mix the wet ingredients in a large mixing bowl. Add the salt and sugar, sift in the flour and bicarbonate of soda and mix well. Give the dough a good knead, adding more flour if it's too sticky. Pop into a clean bowl and leave to sit in a warm spot for about an hour.

To make the filling, heat the oil in a frying pan and add the spring onion first, then the spinach and dill. Sauté, then take off the heat, squeeze any water out and mix in the labneh. Set aside.

Divide the rested dough into 4–6 balls, and roll each ball to a 20 cm (8 in) circle – thin like a pizza base. Divide the filling and place some onto one half of each of the dough rounds. Fold the other side over and seal the sides, pinching the seams to close.

Fry the gözleme in a lightly oiled pan until brown and crispy in parts, then flip to cook the other side. Serve with a wedge of lemon, and some yoghurt to dip if you wish.

Note: *A sweeter-style filling works too. This can be as simple as some butter, ground cinnamon, brown sugar and chopped walnuts. You can roll these up instead of making the pockets – first roll, and then twist that roll into a twirl and fry like that. Sprinkle with some raw sugar.*

Danish koldskål

Koldskål translates to 'cold bowl'. It is a lovely summer dish traditionally made with buttermilk, which I don't have handy very often. However, I do have a lot of milk kefir, so I use that instead and it's pretty similar and a lot healthier. *Koldskål* is so refreshing as a late afternoon or evening snack. We sometimes have it for dinner on hot nights when no one feels like anything much after a large lunch. *Koldskål* is made with uncooked egg yolks. If you are not comfortable with eating raw eggs, you can just leave them out.

<u>SERVES: 2–4</u>

2 egg yolks
2–3 tablespoons sugar
dash of vanilla extract
1 tablespoon lemon juice
1 litre (34 fl oz/4 cups) cold milk kefir
strawberries or blueberries, mashed and
** chopped, to serve**

Whip the egg yolks, sugar, vanilla and lemon juice together really well and then slowly add the cold milk kefir, whisking as you go. That's it!

To serve, put some mashed strawberries or blueberries in the bowl, pour in the liquid, then add some chopped ones on top. Eat immediately – hopefully outside on a warm evening with grass underfoot.

Note: *It's best if you have some* kammerjunker *or* tvebakker, *which are twice-baked cardamom biscuits that you can crumble over the top before eating. You can't easily get them outside of Denmark, but keep your eye out. Dutch rusks, while not the same, can take their place. Or just stick with the berries.*

>>> *more recipes on page 118*

THE MAGIC OF WHEY AND
BUTTER FAT SEPARATION

Kefir pancakes

Basically, these are buttermilk pancakes. You can substitute the plain flour for buckwheat or another gluten-free flour if you like. The night before you want to make these, you can partially mix your batter; you could even leave it a day or two covered and in the fridge. They don't need to be made the night before – I just tend to do it because most mornings I am also filling bento boxes.

300 ml (10 fl oz) milk kefir or yoghurt
200 g (7 oz/1⅓ cups) plain (all-purpose) flour
1 egg
1 teaspoon bicarbonate of soda (baking soda)
pinch of salt
oil or butter, for frying

ADD-INS (BEFORE COOKING)
blueberries or raspberries
generous pinch of ground cinnamon
chocolate chips or banana

If you're starting the batter the night before, combine the milk kefir and flour in a large mixing bowl, cover and allow to sit overnight. Add the remaining ingredients, and any add-ins, just before you cook the pancakes the next day.

Otherwise, on the morning you want to eat them, combine all the ingredients in a mixing bowl, including any add-ins you want to include.

Heat some oil or butter in a frying pan over medium heat, and when hot, ladle the batter into the pan. Flip when the bottom is golden, and remove when cooked on both sides. If you wish, you can put the pancakes on a plate in a warm oven while you cook the rest.

Eat while warm.

Notes: *If you have any leftovers, they freeze pretty well. Reheat in a sandwich press, toaster or microwave another time.*

To turn these into savoury pancakes, omit the sugar and add grated cheese and some spring onion (scallion) and kimchi juice. The kimchi juice and cheese combination is a good one!

Crackers/crispbreads

These play host very delicately to anything you'd like – from goat's curd with see-through slices of persimmon and chives, to labneh with red fennel kraut, marinated mussels with wasabi mayonnaise, or rillettes or mushroom parfait with roast shallots. Consider adding wasabi powder or dulse flakes, or other whole-leaf herbs to these.

250 ml (8½ fl oz/1 cup) milk kefir
few drops of Beet Kvass (page 146) or red brine from a beet kraut (optional)
450 g (1 lb/3 cups) wholemeal (whole-wheat) flour (spelt, buckwheat or other flour of your choice – see notes)
1 teaspoon fine sea salt (plus extra for sprinkling)
125 g (4½ oz) softened butter (optional)
olive oil, for brushing
dukkah or sumac, for sprinkling (optional)

Preheat the oven to 180°C (350°F).

Mix the milk kefir (and if you want a pink cracker, the beet kvass or red brine) with the flour or mix of flours and salt until nicely blended and doughy. Let it rest somewhere warm for 12–24 hours.

Add the butter (if using) by kneading it in. Roll into about four balls and run them through a pasta machine on the lasagne sheet setting. This results in a really fine cracker.

If you don't have a pasta machine, then roll the balls out as thinly as possible with a rolling pin. Cut into squares or long rectangles or whatever shape you'd like – we use a pizza cutter to do this. You can also just leave them in long sheets to keep like that and break as you eat.

Transfer the crackers to a greased baking tray with baking paper on top, and brush them with some olive oil and sprinkle with salt, or other spices like dukkah, or sumac, if you wish.

Bake for about 15 minutes. Store in an airtight container. They'll keep for a few weeks at least.

Notes: *I usually mix my flours purely out of necessity as we always end up with only a quarter of a bag of different lovely flours in the pantry. These crackers are a great way to use those flours up. In the past, I've used a blend of sesame and besan (chickpea) flours or almond meal, spelt and buckwheat.*

We started playing with colour first (the beet kvass addition was one of the results) and then started experimenting with adding lovely herbs as well. Rolling them out extra thin and then putting full herbs in and folding another layer of dough over and re-pressing in the pasta machine is pretty lovely.

You can play around with the amount of liquid you add; just don't make it too wet or it won't roll out as thinly.

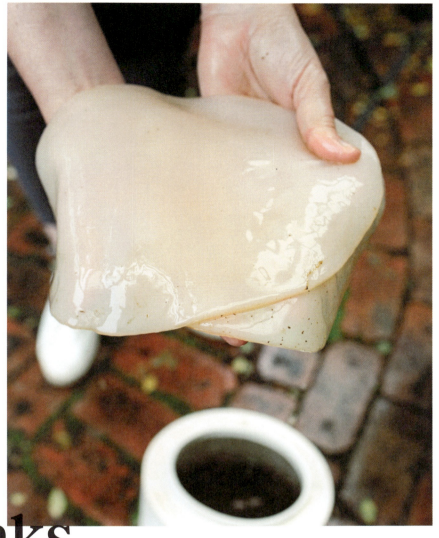

Drinks

If you are looking to eliminate a soda addiction, fermented drinks might be your key to success, as these are little go-to, secret, healthy, refreshing – almost life-changing – drinks. There's a tiny amount of alcohol in fermented drinks, and having a glass at 'wine-o-clock' or in the morning always imparts a healthy, happy feeling. It's a true tonic.

I love all of the common and popular fermented drinks – beer, wine and ciders ... probably a bit too much for my budget, to be honest. I'm a sucker for good packaging and funky designs, and craft brewing has picked up to a point that the shelves are lined with beautiful labels and bottle shapes from all over the world.

But I digress. There are other ways to ferment drinks, whether you use a SCOBY or not. Many DO require a SCOBY, so if you don't have one of those, start with one of the alternatives here until you get your hands on one.

As usual, you'll need your typical measures of courage, intuition, curiosity and optimism. And just in case, the ability to smell when something didn't work, and the heart to give it back to the earth.

You will need to have a few other things of course:

— 2–4 litre (68 fl oz–135 fl oz) jars, a ceramic vat, or a jar or vat with a tap

— muslin (cheesecloth) or other light cloth

— strainer

— funnels

— plastic tubs for mixing and storing

— glass bottles, preferably swing-top.

Be as clean with your preparation as possible without using any harsh antibacterials. Use very hot water to sterilise your jars and crocks. It's best to let them air-dry rather than wiping them.

You could also just run your bottles through the dishwasher, or pour boiling water into them and swish that around. However you do it, get your bottles nice and clean.

Be aware that although glass is lovely, you may prefer to use plastic bottles to avoid dangerous explosions. I choose glass, but use only thick, good-quality bottles. I've only had a couple of breakages and that was because I heated the bottles on the bottom of the oven in a zealous attempt to sterilise them. I recommend you use swing-top bottles. If you are uneasy about explosions, then put the bottles safely out of the way somewhere in a plastic tub. If they explode from within a plastic tub, the mess won't bother you as much. Cleaning up sticky liquid might ruin your *zanmai* (see page 213) a bit, but flying bits of glass do no good to anyone. And don't go putting your bottles out of the way and somewhere warm like on the top of your fridge – a popular place, but it's eye height and a bit too warm. OUCH. Don't do it.

Fermenting with a SCOBY

As I mentioned earlier, SCOBY stands for symbiotic colony of bacteria and yeast. It comes in different forms – kombucha and jun SCOBYs look like floating gel-like mushrooms, while water kefir SCOBYs look like little see-through grains, although they are not a grain at all.

You'll need to get hold of one of these from a friend, a swap meet, online or a shop. It's also possible to grow a SCOBY from the leftovers of an existing bottle of good, living, commercially made kombucha or jun. It's harder with kefir – unless a few little tiny ones slipped through and are in the bottle. No harm in trying.

It's likely you'll end up with a favourite SCOBY not because of the flavour or health benefits you seek, but more likely the amount of work required to get to the end result – how repetitious, how demanding – and how much time you are prepared to give.

SCOBYs are often referred to as 'mothers', but go by many different names around the world. All of these mothers are beautiful, natural life forms. I'm often asked who makes them, or how to make them – they come from nature.

There are a lot of broad statements on the various health benefits these drinks will bring – that they are full of probiotics and healthy yeasts. And lots of people swear their health has improved by drinking their 'buch or kefir. The nutritional benefits or an exact calculation of the various bacteria and yeasts each SCOBY produces is not easily measured because they vary considerably in each environment, home, season and recipe.

There are also claims that it's all a sham. I'm obviously a believer that our relationship to this ferment is real and natural and has been around for aeons. I have seen first hand how it can help digestive systems and wellbeing in general. I've had people from all walks of life call with their story – probably because they heard mine, they were more inclined to share theirs. The most common happy endings are to do with healing difficult and hard to budge (sorry) cases of constipation, as well as lethargy, depression and anxiety.

WHAT KIND OF SCOBY IS FOR YOU?

To begin, here is a very simple summary of what kind of commitment you'll need for each one. Quite like choosing a breed of dog by considering your lifestyle, you will probably also choose your SCOBY by how much time you'd like to put in. Water kefir is very demanding and can start to feel more like an annoying pet than a loving companion – it's a yappy high-maintenance dog, compared to the easygoing labrador that kombucha is. Kombucha and jun don't mind a bit of ignoring; they are a good, forgiving, quiet and strong pet.

They all grow pretty easily. Comfortingly and fascinatingly, this kind of fermentation has also existed alongside humans for a very long time. When you get your first successful batch of water kefir, jun or kombucha, you will probably wonder how the heck something so amazing could have been so absent from your life until now.

FROM LEFT: WATER KEFIR,
KOMBUCHA SCOBY, JUN
SCOBY, MILK KEFIR

KOMBUCHA

Kombucha has a large pancake-shaped mother, and feeds on tea and sugar. It prefers black tea, but you can fiddle around and use other teas successfully. (Avoid teas that have essential oils flavouring them though.) This is probably the most well-known ferment and is readily available at supermarkets – particularly in the US. This is a 7–14 day ferment, and it prefers a warm room. A 1–4 day second ferment allows you to flavour it and can make it very fizzy.

JUN

Jun also has a large pancake-shaped mother, and is fed on green tea and honey. It has a 3–5 day ferment at room temperature. Jun is very mild and light; you can mix your green teas up to find the right flavour for you. Do a second bottle ferment for 1–3 days.

WATER KEFIR

Water kefir's mother is often called a grain because of the shape. These are little gel-like crystals, fed on sugar and water and various minerals. It has a 48-hour first ferment and a 24-hour second ferment. It's demanding because of this continuous rotation, but can produce great flavours and become very fizzy. Water kefir is higher in lactic acid bacteria, as opposed to kombucha and jun, which have more acetic acid.

MILK KEFIR

Milk kefir's mother is also called a grain purely for its shape – but it's probably more like a stretchy sea-like cauliflower or something. It feeds on milk and can get very effervescent. It's known as the champagne of milk. There is a 24–48 hour first ferment, and an optional second ferment if you're after fizz or want more of the lactose to be eaten up and converted. Milk kefir is healthy, delicious, and in fact, a personal favourite. (Details for this are in the Milk & dairy chapter, see page 102 onwards.)

ON BUYING YOUR DRINK

With fermented drinks – like anything else – look at the ingredients. If they list the exact kinds of bacteria and yeast, they are most likely added from a manufactured powder. There shouldn't need to be any ingredients in the drink that you wouldn't add at home. Many of the drinks in shop fridges have been pasteurised or over-brewed to make them transportable and saleable under all the different food laws. Unless it's been made traditionally, and not pasteurised, the microbial diversity will be much smaller. It's better to have the real thing, made by you, so you know what's in it. You will get the whole, rich array of natural yeasts and bacteria. When it is so easy to brew, grows like crazy and gives a beautiful product, why would you choose another way?

JUN & KOMBUCHA

You can leave jun and kombucha for weeks without feeding, and pop them into the fridge if you need a rest. (Do this only for very long breaks, as there is a chance you will lose a lot of the diverse bacteria and yeast by doing this.) This independence is quite an attractive attribute, especially when you have a kitchen full of other needy ferments and you also have an actual real job and life to attend to.

Jun has a gentler flavour, and is also therefore easier to imbibe with your own flavours. Jun is not as available in shops just yet, which makes it a unique ferment. It could have something to do with the price of good honey (and let's keep it that way because honey is so precious). The jun mother is a little lighter in colour, is brighter and more porous than the kombucha mother and therefore more pleasant to work with. (I actually feel like biting it every time I squeeze it.)

Both jun and kombucha are perhaps initially a bit off-putting for some people, but somehow once you're alone and get to know them, they become very charming. Seriously, people have trouble throwing their excess out at times!

One part of the charm is that they grow to the air space you give them. Think of that! So if you put one in a small jar, it will soon cover the surface of that jar. If you put one in a bath full of sweet tea, it will do the same. My eldest daughter grew one for fun in a shallow tub. She pulled the layers off and dried them out with a view to paint on them like a canvas or a hide; the problem was that they return to life when they get wet … so back to the … fermenting tank.

And where do they come from? Like a lot of history, there's not a really reliable source, and the stories are quite vague because they really have been around for a long time. It seems as though they come from Asia, where there is a long history with tea. That makes sense to me. Kombu in Japanese refers to seaweeds, and cha refers to tea, so it could be that the SCOBY looked so sea-like that it was named after the seaweed? Another story is that there was a Korean doctor called Kombu (well, Kon-mu was the Japanese translation of his name) who prescribed this elixir to Japanese Emperor Ingyo in the fifth century. Legend says that it was so successful that the Emperor named the drink after the doctor – Kombu-cha.

HOW TO GROW A MOTHER

With a real living kombucha or jun, growing a mother should be easy. If you don't have any, buy a living brew (a proper one, not one that vaguely calls itself a 'probiotic drink'). Drink half of it and then sit your bottle out without the lid, but covered with a bit of cloth in your cupboard, where it's nice and warm and dark, and try to forget about it for a while. (I've grown mothers by accident with the lid on too – even one left rolling under the seat of my car. A gift!) Your kombucha or jun mother will appear – a gelatinous wafer that you can be proud of. That's your SCOBY.

BUYING A MOTHER

When buying a mother make sure that it's not from a fridge and that it comes with at least half a cup of actual kombucha or jun tea. Otherwise you could have trouble with your brew later on. Always better to buy a good-quality SCOBY than something that has been 'asleep' in the fridge for who knows how long.

SOME GENERAL TIPS

— As all the drinks become quite acidic, use only glass, lead-free ceramic or stainless steel vessels to ferment in.

— For kombucha and jun, remember to always keep the pH down with some brew from your last batch. Maintaining the right pH sounds difficult, but it's naturally very low. You can taste it. If your 'buch or jun is sweet after a reasonable fermenting time then it's not working. It may just be that you need to leave it for a longer time, but if no fermentation is occurring, eventually mould will grow. That's a sure-fire way to know that it's not working.

— Use the tap on your jar, or a turkey-baster-style sucker, to suck some out to test it. A pH meter is cheap, but I've never bothered for home use. If you are very into fermenting it might be fun to have one. The pH should lie somewhere between 2.5 and 4.6. Any lower and you have yourself a vinegar, and that is safe too – but higher than 4.6 and it's not fermented. And you'd know it by tasting it.

— Little annoying vinegar bugs love kombucha and jun. You don't want them – keep your brew covered well by securing a cloth with a rubber band, and keeping it dry and clean.

— When you give a SCOBY away, always include some of the liquid – at least 250 ml (8½ fl oz/1 cup).

— We have received many nervous calls from customers before they drink their kombucha or jun – or even eat sauerkraut – because they're worried that they don't know what amount to 'take'. I'm happy to answer calls and help out, but when did natural, unprocessed, fermented food become scary? Does anybody realise what goes into a shelf-stable cake or a can of soft drink?

— Yes, you do need to go slowly if you know you have gut health issues, low immunity or a lot of allergies. Start with a shot or two in the morning, and again at night. Your body may need time to adjust to new bacteria, acetic acid and yeasts. I've heard of people coming out in rashes and feeling nauseous from drinking too much of it. This is a time to drink in moderation for sure – use common sense. I suppose that is also why I prefer to recommend the continuous brew system (page 128) – you take small amounts, even just a bottle at a time, rather than bottling up a few at once.

KOMBUCHA
SECOND
FERMENT

Continuous brew kombucha or jun

I've started you off with 1 litre (34 fl oz/4 cups) of water, but listed a 4 L (135 fl oz) tapped vat because it's gentler to start off small with a new mother and build her up to a larger batch. It'll take about 2 weeks to get your first batch out.

On the second round, double the recipe to 2 litres (68 fl oz/8 cups). Increase until you've got the perfect amount for the rhythm of your life and the vat size that satiates your 'buch or jun appetite.

As the brew gets low, make enough sweet tea (or honey green tea) to top your vessel up, let it cool then add it to your vat by gently pulling the mother aside as you pour in the tea. The mother will soon thicken up and you'll love watching her grow. Now and then I recommend you pull the top layers off to allow the healthy young mother to work. Let the old lady retire – pop her out in the garden or compost.

A constant supply can be achieved by keeping a simple rotation: drawing from it, feeding it again, bottling it, flavouring that, and topping up.

Preparation time: 15 minutes
Fermentation time: 1–2 weeks
Equipment: 4 L (135 fl oz) tapped vat, muslin (cheesecloth), bottles for storing

1 litre (34 fl oz/4 cups) water (see notes)
55 g (2 oz) sugar or honey (see notes)
2 tablespoons black tea or honey green tea (see notes)
125 ml (4 fl oz/½ cup) ready-made kombucha or jun
1 kombucha or jun mother

Unless you are cold-brewing your tea, heat the water to about 80°C (175°F), add it to the vat, dissolve the sugar or honey in the water, add the tea and brew this to the strength you like. Let it come to room temperature before removing the tea and adding the already-made kombucha or jun and the mother. I always like to taste the tea at this point, so I have a marker to go by for later on in the week when it should be turning sour.

Cover it up with muslin or other cloth, and secure it to dissuade the bugs. Regardless, they may even come and sit ON your muslin if you've wet it in the process, so be careful and make sure your cloth stays dry and clean.

Put it in a warm spot, and out of direct sunlight. Room temperature is great, but be aware that it will sour much faster in warmer conditions, and that while it will ferment in cooler environments, it may take longer. If you live in a cold climate or have a cold house you may want to consider getting a heat mat. The warmer it is, the faster it will ferment. It will probably take 1–2 weeks to get to the sour point you are looking for. My brew right now is so healthy and happy that it gets sour in days – sometimes only 3–5 days. You get a faster batch using continuous brew than you would with just a jar system (see pages 130 or 132).

If you have used a tapped vat, you can pour from it any time you like to get an idea of the changing flavours.

When it's perfect, or when you are happy with it, bottle it up into the bottles you have bought or collected.

Then add your second ferment flavours – this is the part that is most fun (see page 130).

Notes: *Water from your tap will do (because you are heating it), but you are far better off using a better source as it's preferable to only heat it hot enough to brew the tea and dissolve the sugar or honey. If you choose to cold-brew, then rainwater, filtered or spring-fed is best. You could make a slurry of hot tea and sugar and add cold water to make the right amount so you don't have to wait as long for the mixture to cool.*

Coconut sugar, rapadura, raw organic, or any other simple sugar is fine. Don't even think of using artificial sweeteners. Honey is okay for kombucha, lots of people use it, but if you use good, raw honey, then the bacteria and yeast in that honey, once mixed with water – basically mead – may interact too much. Jun tea feeds on honey, so choose jun if honey is your preference, or you have a hive and honey is in abundance.

Cold-brew teas make a fabulous kombucha or jun, and once you've experi-fermented a bit I would highly recommend having a play with the many and varied natural herbal teas, rooibos and green tea. You can use other kinds of tea with amazing flavour success, but avoid the kind of tea that has essential oils in it, which may wreak havoc with your culture.

Kombucha likes the tannins and polyphenols in tea, so it's best to use a mixture of proper tea and herbal tea (if you want to use herbal tea), or at least use plain black tea every couple of brews. This is because herbal teas that don't contain any actual tea are actually tisanes – a herbal soaking rather than from the tea plant Camellia sinensis. Suitable teas include white tea, English breakfast, darjeeling, assam and ceylon. Greens include sencha and oolong.

I like to use loose tea, but tea bags or balls are great too. You can find empty tea bags in Asian food or specialty shops, which are great for making your own mixes. Best choose the kind that aren't bleached if you can find them.

You'll know the mother has started growing when you see a foggy layer on the top of your water a few days after you've begun. You can poke it to check if it is cellulose and forming, but best leave it alone until it's a bit thicker.

Stringy bits may form, particularly down the bottom. That's just yeast – sometimes you'll find this happens in your bottled 'buch too. To avoid that a little, I like to strain my batches as I bottle. It is a living elixir, so bits and pieces turn up now and then, and that is the bewitching thing about fermented, living brews.

The mother won't always live on the top; she may float down, diagonally or lower – but if that happens usually one will form on the top anyway. If nothing happens and after a week or so your tea is still sweet, you may have to work on repairing things. (You should have taken better care of your mother!)

Second ferment

Feel free to get creative with second fermenting. This is where all of your own personal favourite flavours and experience with tastes comes in. Rhubarb and basil? Throw a bit in! Not strong enough, or too strong? Try more or less next time if you are inspired by that flavour.

I apologise for how loose this all seems for a recipe book, but the variances in every part of fermentation are very real and so an actual detailed recipe wouldn't always work anyway.

You need to use your foodie intuition.

You don't need a lot of fruit per litre. I've even had new SCOBYs grow over my fruit concoctions within days before I realised. There it was making another batch of kombucha already so I had to strain and re-bottle to get the fizz I was looking for.

Add your flavours (see page 143 for some ideas), then lid your bottles to encourage carbonation, and let sit for a few days, until it's fizzy enough for you. Beware though: it can become very fizzy at this stage, and you must promise to use a flip-top lid, or at least a thick, good-quality glass bottle. Explosions can happen and accidents from these glass bombs aren't pretty.

When it's fizzy enough, pop it into the fridge to slow further fermentation, and drink when cold. It will keep for as long as you think it's delicious, though I shouldn't like to drink it after more than 6 months.

Kombucha: jar system

Rather than use the continuous brew system, many people prefer to use a jar or crock and then bottle each batch up in almost its entirety each time. This can be a lovely way to get quite a few bottles in your fridge at once. Don't forget to keep a couple of inches of brewed 'buch each time. The recipe is pretty much the same as for a continuous brew, and so are the rules.

Preparation time: 15 minutes
Fermentation time: 7–14 days
Equipment: 2+ L (68+ fl oz) glass jar or crock, cloth (muslin/cheesecloth or a light towel), bottles for storing

>>> *continued on page 132*

1 litre (34 fl oz/4 cups) water
55 g (2 oz/¼ cup) organic raw (demerara) sugar
2 tablespoons black tea, or 2 black tea bags
60 ml (2 fl oz/¼ cup) ready-made kombucha from an earlier batch
1 kombucha mother

Heat the water, add the sugar and stir until dissolved. Add the tea and leave to brew until it is room temperature. Remove the tea or tea bags. Pour the mixture into the jar with the ready-made kombucha and the kombucha mother. Cover with some muslin or cloth and pop a rubber band over to secure it.

Sit on the kitchen bench and keep it covered, if only with a tea (dish) towel, to keep sunlight out if you have a bright bench. A temperature of about 18°C (64°F) is perfect. The warmer it is, the faster it will ferment, but a timeframe of 7 days is average. During this time the mother should have grown to cover the air space allowed, and started to grow another underneath it. The sugar will be eaten and the tea will become sour, almost vinegar-like.

Strain it now, making sure to save some for your next batch, and bottle your kombucha – you can add fruit and let it sit out for a second fermentation in the bottle, which will result in a fizzier and (I think) more delicious drink. I've listed some nice combinations to use for second fermentation at the end of this section (page 143).

Notes: *Watch it because, as per the previous recipe, it can get so fizzy that it can become explosive and break the bottle quite violently and unexpectedly. Definitely use thick, good-quality bottles, preferably swing-top, or burp the bottle to let air out during the second fermentation. It may only need a couple of days, although sometimes it'll need more. The more sugar and fruit you put into the kombucha, the more*

carbonation (and alcohol) will be produced, so keep that in mind. The alcohol level is usually relatively low – about 0.5–1.5% – but it can get a bit higher with fruits high in sugar. Know that with most fermented products small amounts of alcohol do exist. If you have sensitivity, you'll feel it straight away.

When you tire of your kombucha, and want a long break, pop it with some of its liquid into an airtight container in the fridge to put it 'to sleep'. It should wake up just fine as long as there is liquid there. You can end up with a hotel – a jar full of mothers waiting to be given to friends.

Jun: jar system

Jun and kombucha are really very similar, with only a few small differences: jun tea ferments more quickly, feeds on green tea and honey, and ferments well at cooler temperatures. There are many blends of green tea available, and as it's a lighter flavour than other teas, the ones you add can really make a difference.

Using honey rather than sugar rids your brew of any potential disaccharide residue from sugar so jun is preferable for those on the GAPS (gut and psychology syndrome) diet, for example.

Preparation time: 15 minutes
Fermentation time: 3–5 days
Equipment: 2+ L (68+ fl oz) glass jar or crock, cloth (muslin/cheesecloth or a light towel), bottles for storing

2 tablespoons green tea, or 3 tea bags
1 litre (34 fl oz/4 cups) boiling water
115 g (4 oz/⅓ cup) organic raw honey
1 jun mother
125 ml (4 fl oz/½ cup) ready-made jun tea

THE
MORE
DELICATE
JUN
MOTHER

In the jar, brew your green tea as you would black tea for kombucha (page 130), and after the water has cooled somewhat, mix in the honey. When the mixture has cooled further, remove the tea and add your jun mother and ready-made jun tea. Cover with some muslin and pop a rubber band over this to secure it.

This will ferment in about 3–5 days, sometimes more, but keep an eye on it as it could get a bit sour. Bottle it up, add your second ferment ingredients (see page 143) and let sit for another day or two until carbonated. I don't always add extra flavours to this as I love it as it is. There is a slight meady flavour to jun, and because it's light, the second ferment flavours seem to penetrate it easily.

Notes: *If your jun over-ferments and is very acidic, keep it for vinegar, or use it as a vinegar in a huge batch of Fire tonic (page 158). It's also great poured over hair in lieu of conditioner. You can also dehydrate your SCOBY and eat it* *(see below). My kids love it, but I have to remind them of how many SCOBYs they are eating and to keep it to a small amount. They're better than a bag of lollies, but I do think about how they rehydrate in their tummies when they are eating their third piece.*

DEHYDRATING THE SCOBY

The first option is to cut it into small pieces and then marinate it in a sugar syrup for about 24 hours. Dehydrate the pieces until they are a texture you like.

Or if you don't want to wait that long, mix a combination of sugar and ground cinnamon, to taste. Remember, you are dehydrating so you don't want the cinnamon to be too strong, as it will get stronger as the bits get smaller. Put the SCOBYs into the sugar mixture as though you were crumbing them. Place into your dehydrator on 40°C (105°F) for about 12 hours. You could also dry out slowly overnight in the oven, under 50°C (122°F). Check them halfway, turn them over and see how they are going. Depending on their thickness they may need less or more time. Store in an airtight container and they'll last for ages.

You could also marinate them first, and make them savoury like jerky. Try using kimchi paste or a mixture of chilli and sugar.

Last, to make a dog treat, you could dehydrate the SCOBYs until they are a little dry but still pliable, then roll them up and dehydrate until they are really dry and crisp, then dip them in bacon or chicken fat and dehydrate some more. The only dog that doesn't like them is mine, but she really isn't food driven. If you have a dog that gulps everything in one mouthful, then make little bite-sized pieces to use as treats, otherwise the SCOBY might come back out as a WHOLE SCOBY. Yikes.

STORING FOR LATER OR TAKING A BREAK

You can get overwhelmed, sick of it or too busy. That's fine. Don't put your SCOBY in the fridge, unless you want a really long break of 6 months or more. People do have success putting them in the fridge, but sometimes a weird thing happens where after the first successful batch, they do another and it becomes mouldy because its bacteria and yeast make-up has changed. I'd sooner pass mine on to someone and get a new one when I'm ready again. Instead, make up a sugar–tea solution and keep it in a dark area. If you have several SCOBYs going you can pop them all into the same jar. You might end up with a jar-full – a 'hotel' (see the image on page 124). Just leave it for a while, and maybe make a new solution now and then to feed them.

WATER KEFIR

Water kefir grains in their natural state are a beautiful kind of gelatinous crystal, but make no mistake – as I've mentioned, the word 'grain' refers to its shape and nothing more. To be precise it is a complex polysaccharide in which bacteria and yeasts exist in a symbiotic matrix. The main players here are lactic acid, acetic acid and yeasts. Good yeasts.

To make this work we need to feed them sugar, which they eat and convert to lactic acid, alcohol and carbon dioxide. The alcohol is only in a small amount, but nevertheless take note: the ability for the yeasts to convert the sugar to alcohol is real, so unless that is your goal, avoid making kefir purely with juices. The amount of alcohol you'll produce will still be very low – no more than 2–3% per cent at its sweetest, which is not the same as having a boozy drink. You'd have to drink 4 litres (a gallon) of the stuff for it to be of much consequence, which you just wouldn't be able to do as it tends to have a diuretic effect.

I think we need to be a bit more sanguine about alcohol. It's not necessarily the enemy and is present in a lot of fermented products in small amounts.

That said, I also think it would be a shame to add refined juices to water kefir. Fresh pulpy ones you've made yourself? Yes. Even better are whole pieces of fruit.

In keeping with fermenting's spontaneous nature, each batch will differ in some way. Our commercial batches do and that is part of water kefir's allure. The environment, conditions and what the SCOBY is fed changes the results accordingly. Once you've found your perfect flavour and technique, reduce the variables. You should be able to expect a consistent flavour with only slight nuances in the end product.

There's no need to tell you that kefir is my favourite of the watery ferments (after wine) to drink. Most people seem to like it, and if they don't, I can usually concoct a flavour that they'll enjoy. I've personally seen people fix constipation, hangovers, exhaustion and alcohol cravings, as well as queasy tummies, with this. It's a curative drink any time of the day or night – particularly the gingery kefirs, which are so nice for your digestion.

Go easy for your first couple of tries, taking a small glass first and building from there. We have a bottle on our dinner table most nights now and the kids love it because it is one of the few options for fizzy drink, and they no longer think of it as a 'healthy' thing. It is a digestif actually, and they don't know it.

USING WATER GRAINS FOR MILK & MILK GRAINS FOR WATER

You can use your milk kefir grains to make water kefir and vice versa, but only for a few times, and they need to be refreshed and fed properly after a couple of rounds. It's best to source the culture for the drink you are trying to make. There are successful stories online of this, but every time I use my milk kefir grains to add life to an apple juice or grape juice, I feel a bit guilty and swap them back to milk pretty quickly. They don't love it, but I have used some sweet juice to revitalise the milk grains overnight when they seem a bit sluggish, and they do make a lovely mild apple or grape cider.

A FEW TIPS

— Kefir loves ginger. It naturally carries a lot of yeast and lactic bacteria, and your SCOBY loves these. Kefir can certainly ferment well without ginger, but feeding it some fresh ginger now and then will make it very happy.

— Kefir loves lemon, and not just the juice. Be sure to use unwaxed lemons. If you can't get them, soak your lemons in hot water to get some of the wax off. Remember to get boxes of them when they're in season. Preserve them in salt etc. for eating (see page 79), but also for your kefir-making life. To do this, spend just an hour each season preserving them by firstly zesting them all and then halving them and juicing them. Pour the juice into ice cube trays – you'll need a lot – and when they are frozen, put them into a container in your freezer. Pop the lemon zest into zip-lock bags, push the air out, and freeze. Add these to your kefir and other drinks all year long.

>>> continued on page 137

— Kefir needs minerals and calcium, which you can get from a clean (boiled) egg shell, some coral or an oyster shell. You don't want too much, just a tiny piece and not every time. I've heard of people using mineral drops and calcium drops, but have never needed to resort to them.

— If you use chlorinated water, nothing bad will happen the first time, but it will show eventually, by the grains not growing, or growing slowly or even shrinking. Keep an eye on your grains to monitor this. If you only have chlorinated tap water, leave it in an open bucket for 24 hours to rid it of some of the chlorine, or boil it and let it cool to room temperature.

— Iron or calcium-heavy water is not good for long-term kefir making. The best water in my opinion is rainwater.

— This is not an exact science; use your intuition, get to know your grains in your particular environment and don't be scared to fiddle around with the recipe. The grains sometimes get tired and may require more of this or that.

— If it's extremely bright and sunny where you'd like to keep your water kefir, just put a tea (dish) towel over it to keep the light out. However, kefir grains do love a sun bath. So in an ordinary kitchen, leave as is, and now and then pop them in the sun on purpose, as they like being warm like that. Watching them travel up and down the jar with the sun on them is quite hypnotic.

Water kefir: basic first ferment

Even though I say it's my preferred drink, I can see why no one really loves to make it. In fact, I'm certain that our business started because I would teach people to make their own, but they would come back a few short weeks later to say that they'd rather pay for it than make it.

It's very easy to make, but it is repetitive – the first ferment is 48 hours, the second ferment is 24 hours, so you never really get a day off. If water kefir becomes your thing, you'll just need to gain some confidence in keeping it alive and happy while you are having a break from it.

The first ferment is more about feeding your kefir SCOBY than creating a gorgeous flavour. Your grains need to be strong in order to produce a healthy-tasting drink and can be affected by the smallest changes. The second ferment, however, is where the art and fun is found and where you make it fizzy and delicious.

Preparation time: ↓20 minutes
Fermentation time: 48 hours, plus a second fermentation of 24 hours
Equipment: 2+L (68+ fl oz) jar, swing-top or lidded bottles for storing

1 litre (34 fl oz/4 cups) water (preferably spring, filtered or rain)
2–4 tablespoons water kefir grains (adjust according to their strength)
55 g (2 oz/¼ cup) organic raw (demerara) sugar (see notes overleaf)
pinch of aluminium-free bicarbonate of soda (baking soda)
¼ teaspoon molasses
2 slices organic lemon with rind, washed well
2 slices ginger, unpeeled and washed well
dried organic fruit (I recommend 1 date and 1 dried fig – see notes overleaf)

Add the water and sugar to the clean jar. If you'd prefer, you can heat some of the water up first, stir in the sugar until dissolved, then mix this into the cool water to bring the temperature down. Alas, I am lazy: I just add the sugar, give it a good hard stir and my kefir forgives me.

Add the remaining ingredients, and give it a gentle stir with a wooden spoon. Secure with a lid that will make it airtight – kefir likes an anaerobic environment.

Large jars that have plastic screw-on lids or flip-top lids are great for this. (If you'd like to keep the alcohol down as low as possible, don't lid it, but cover with a cloth or a secured paper towel instead. You just may not get the carbonation as easily later on, and the grains might not grow as quickly.)

Sit it somewhere with a consistent temperature of about 18–21°C (65–70°F) for 48 hours.

Using a strainer, pour the water kefir into a bowl or jug, remove the fruit (see notes) and ginger from the grains, and place your grains in a jar for another batch. (Yes, that's right, you'll need to make another batch now, or feed them if not.)

Bottle the young water kefir, add your flavours and leave it to second ferment (see next recipe). If you're trying to avoid alcohol, pop it straight in the fridge after adding your low-sugar flavours.

Notes: If you prefer your water kefir sweeter, you can add more sugar – up to 75 g (2¾ oz/⅓ cup). Wait until your grains have grown so you have spares before you experiment with coconut sugar or other natural sweeteners. Don't use raw honey as the bacteria may wreak havoc with the grains – some people use it successfully but I don't recommend it. If you use a darker sugar like coconut sugar or rapadura then you won't need molasses.

This is very important: make sure the dried fruit you use is organic and not coated in waxes, oils or sulphates. Experiment with dried fruit – especially when you have extra grains to play around with. Other dried fruits, such as sultanas (golden raisins), work if you don't have a fig or date.

The fruit you remove from the first ferment can sometimes be used again or, if not, is perfect for blending into raw protein balls, for example. It's pretty amazing to see a dried fig puffed up and fizzy when you open it. Chickens, pigs, goats and other animals love them as well.

Water kefir: second ferment (the fun part)

Now that you've bottled your water kefir after the first ferment of 48 hours, you can flavour it. This 24-hour period is called the 'second fermentation'. Try not to add anything that is too high in sugar, like apple juice for example. The sugar will still convert to alcohol at this point; the more sugar, the more carbonation as well, so that's another reason you don't want too much sugar. (Read on for more on explosions.) The second ferment is when it will become fizzy and divine. If this doesn't happen, then leave it out a bit longer, checking on it frequently.

I've included one recipe for a water kefir second ferment below – flick to page 143 for more flavour ideas.

Fig & ginger water kefir second ferment

At The Fermentary, we use about 10 ml (¼ fl oz) fresh ginger juice and 20 ml (¾ fl oz) lemon juice per litre (34 fl oz) for this kefir. Before I made it commercially, I would simply slip a finger of fresh ginger, a wedge of lemon and maybe another dried fig into each 1 litre (34 fl oz) bottle, then I'd let it steep, leaving the fruit proudly in the bottle when serving.

Add the ginger and lemon – either juiced or whole (and maybe a fig) – to each bottle. Seal and let them sit at room temperature for about 24 hours. (A second fermentation can be achieved in the fridge, but may take a day or two longer to achieve the same amount of effervescence.) After the second ferment, refrigerate and drink.

GLASS

Remember that you need to use a thick, very good quality bottle and only leave it out for 24 hours to second ferment because it will KEEP FERMENTING. If you add too much sugar or very sweet fruit, the kefir will become more alcoholic and highly carbonated. At best, it will pop out of the bottle like champagne, but it has also been known to explode – sending a sorry mess of glass all through the fridge. Until you are quite familiar with your recipe, it may be a good idea to use plastic bottles, or at least one plastic bottle as a gauge – when that gets completely puffed out, then you know it's time to put the bottles in the fridge. Always open carefully by burping them a bit first.

STORING YOUR GRAINS FOR LATER OR HAVING A REST

Your grains will grow rapidly when they're healthy and settled. If you don't gift them to a friend, or make larger batches often, you may want to save them for when you do want to make a huge batch. There are a few different methods for doing this.

— Dehydrate them by laying them out on a screen in the sun, or between some paper towels. My preference is to use a dehydrator. Keep the temperature below 40°C (105°F), and they'll be dry within a day. You can then sprinkle them on yoghurt with granola. I had a friend who enjoyed chewing on them when she was hiking in Asia. I find them a bit chewy and the texture becomes gel-like when it rehydrates, but they may do the job of keeping your gut healthy when you can't access anything else.

— Strain them and sprinkle some raw sugar on them. Pop them into a zip-lock bag and into the freezer – only for a few months.

— Probably the best way to have a rest is to simply keep them in jars resting on the bench, feeding them but not making anything out of them. I just make up a mixture of water, sugar, molasses, a couple of slices of ginger ... just as though I'm making a batch, but using less water and more grains per jar. You could keep looking after them like this for a while without any trouble by refreshing the water now and then and adding some egg shell and a few dates occasionally.

EXCESS

When you have a surplus, a great thing to do is to mix them in with your pet's food; they're a great source of probiotics for them, too. City dogs need this particularly as they aren't exposed to as much bacteria as they probably should be – unless you feed them only raw food or let them eat road kill, poop or all the things they are naturally inclined to eat. Start off with one or two grains mixed in per meal and go from there. Pigs love to eat them. Worms only like them a little bit. You can also add some grains to the compost to increase its bacterial diversity.

There are quite a few people out there making soaps and other skin products by mixing and blending SCOBYs, or tanning or drying them with the intention of using it for clothing or bags.

WATER KEFIR
GRAINS

MIXING YOUR DRINKS

Alcohol aside, playing with your finished water kefir is worthwhile. Kefir is a beverage worthy of your mixing efforts. Simply adding ice and some mint, for example, is satisfying enough to feel like you are being indulgent. That's what a drink in the evening is for me – about indulgence, treating myself to something that isn't necessary, a bit naughty even, and not for the kids, just for me. I like wine, but if we are at a music festival or something outdoors and the sun is shining then this is my preferred sipper. Add some vermouth or a touch of gin or vodka and a few sprigs of mint or sage, and you're onto a winner. We have several lovely wine bars in Melbourne playing around with water kefir, using our own raspberry kefir with Campari or in a slushy to make a margarita-style drink. A mint and lime kefir makes something like a mojito, with or without the alcohol.

Having warned you about them dying off and not using chlorinated water, or sulphured fruits, or waxed lemons, I have to say that water kefir grains are also pretty tough little things. I was renting a place on 12 acres when I first moved back to Australia, and as the business grew the cottage out the back filled with more and more fridges. One day, I was taking a huge jar of grains out to shelve for a few days (having a break!) when I tripped and fell, smashing the jar of grains everywhere – all over the gravel driveway. I assessed the situation: the gravel, gel-like water kefir grains and glass.

I picked up the glass as well as I could, in tears. But there was no way I could pick up each grain. There were thousands of them. It started to rain and they sat there in their gel-like happy state. I felt guilty every time I walked out to my car and saw them. After a week of sunny days they had happily kind of disappeared, mixed in with the gravel. I drove my car over it every day. Phew, out of sight, out of mind. But alas, the next time it rained, and every time it rained for months – until I moved away from that house actually – those grains reappeared. I'm sure you wouldn't be able to make kefir out of them, but they didn't disappear and it killed me to see that. I wonder if they are still appearing from time to time, if the chooks finally got to them or if the owners of the property have seen them and wondered what in the world I put on their driveway.

SECOND FERMENT FLAVOUR IDEAS FOR KOMBUCHA, JUN & WATER KEFIR

Make a diary of what you are doing so that when you get a really good batch you can replicate it as much as the brew allows. Use tape and write the brewing date on it – particularly with jun and 'buch.

Kombucha and jun have the extra element of using tea for flavour. This can make a very sophisticated, subtle beverage worth playing around with.

These amounts are for 1 litre (34 fl oz) bottles and are suggestions only – add or take away as you please. I've grouped them into ideas that would go with each tea. If you are using a flavoured tea like a mixture of fennel and black, where the fennel is just for flavour, make sure you use the full amount of black. On top of the specific suggestions on page 144, you can add all the combinations to a water kefir second ferment or an infusion; just ignore the tea and add the remaining ingredients to your bottle.

TO GREEN TEA KOMBUCHA OR JUN ADD:

— 1 tablespoon pomegranate molasses, or to taste

— juice of 1 orange and a few cardamom pods

— 5+ raspberries (fresh/frozen) and 1 lime wedge

— 1 slice of honeydew melon, 1 slice of cucumber and 1 mint sprig

— 1–2 strawberries

— 2 basil leaves and a squeeze of lemon juice

— 2 pieces of rhubarb and 2–3 basil leaves

— ½ slice of dried persimmon, 1 slice of pear, 1 slice of ginger and a squeeze of lemon.

TO PLAIN ENGLISH BREAKFAST TEA KOMBUCHA OR JUN ADD:

— a handful of mint leaves, 2 wedges of lime (with peel) or the juice of ½ lime.

TO BLACK TEA KOMBUCHA OR JUN ADD:

— 2–3 cubes of pineapple and 1 slice of orange

— 1 strand of saffron, pinch of cayenne pepper and 1 large piece of pineapple.

TO A MIXTURE OF WHITE AND BLACK OR BLACK AND MULBERRY LEAF TEA KOMBUCHA OR JUN ADD:

— 1–2 pieces of grapefruit, or the juice of ½ grapefruit.

TO ASSAM TEA KOMBUCHA OR JUN ADD:

— 2 slices of orange and 5 blueberries.

TO BLACK, GREEN OR ASSAM TEA ADD:

— 2 slices of pear and 1 slice of ginger.

TO WHITE TEA KOMBUCHA OR JUN ADD:

— 2 slices of watermelon, 1–2 wedges of lime and a couple of basil leaves (or even chopped basil stalks).

TO A MIXTURE OF WHITE AND GREEN TEA KOMBUCHA OR JUN ADD:

— 5+ blackberries and a few sage leaves.

TO A MIXTURE OF WHITE AND BLACK TEA KOMBUCHA OR JUN ADD:

— 2+ slices of peach and a couple of mint leaves.

TO WATER KEFIR OR AN INFUSION ADD:

— ½ peach and 1 cut fingerlime (that's an Australian native – if you can get some, do, otherwise use 1 wedge of grapefruit or ½ lime)

— 1 slice of watermelon or some basil leaves (or both) with either 1 wedge of lime, a rosemary sprig or a few mint sprigs

— ½ nectarine and a few juniper berries

— 1 hibiscus flower and 1 wedge of lime

— 2 tablespoons pomegranate seeds or 1 tablespoon pomegranate molasses

— 1 wedge of melon and 1 teaspoon coriander seeds or 1 coriander (cilantro) root

— 1 tablespoon rose petals, palmful of raspberries and ½ vanilla bean

— a handful of blackberries and ½ peach

— 3 cherries and 1 vanilla bean (re-use)

— a wedge of lemon, slice of ginger, 1 coriander (cilantro) root and 1 small chilli

— a little bunch of elderflowers or elderflower cordial, to taste

— 5 slices of cucumber and a few mint sprigs

— ½ orange and 10 blueberries

— 1 chopped apple and 1 cinnamon stick

— a handful of cranberries and 1 star anise.

INFUSIONS

You could also add the water kefir ideas to water to infuse it with gorgeous flavour. For hardier things such as elderflower, steep in boiling water, then allow to cool. Let the flavoured water sit for a few hours and drink as is. Or you could add a flavoured water to a whey soda (see the recipe for Ginger-'wheyed' recipe on the opposite page, for example). With whey sodas, be generous with your infusion ingredients because on the whole and by definition, infusions don't make the water overly sweet; the flavours are lovely and subtle.

Fermented drinks (no SCOBY)

I know I'm enthusiastic and always say how easy it is to ferment all the things, but with the recipes that follow, you can't argue. Wild yeasts can be found all around us. Experi-ferment a little bit – anything with a white bloom on it has yeast (think grapes, plums, berries, young pine cones and juniper berries). Capture this yeast and use it!

The hardest part about making your own fizzy drink is finding the huge jars, stirring often and waiting. The drinks in this section promise to provide a lot. They:

— are delicious and satisfying

— are a very cheap way to get friendly bacteria inside you, get your gut sorted, get your fermentation kick

— make great projects for kids

— offer an easy way to make homemade fizz for all the people in your life – or maybe just for you.

Ginger-'wheyed'

Here it is, a recipe that uses whey as a starter for naturally carbonated soda. If you've been to Switzerland (or not) you may have heard of Rivella, their national favourite fizzy drink, originally made using whey as a starter. Every country has a version of a fizzy drink that starts with what's readily available. Switzerland – with all the whey left from cheesemaking – naturally has a whey drink.

Preparation time: 10 minutes
Fermentation time: 2+ days
Equipment: 1 large jar with an air-lock system, or enough bottles to hold up to 3 L (101 fl oz) liquid (see notes)

fresh ginger, finely grated, to taste (from a thumb-sized piece to a whole hand, depending on how hot you want it)
150 g (5½ oz) honey or sugar
pinch of salt
juice of 1–2 lemons
50 ml (1¾ fl oz) fresh whey (you only need a little to kickstart it – see notes)
2 litres (68 fl oz/8 cups) water (see notes)

Mix the ginger with the honey, salt, lemon juice and whey until the salt has dissolved.

Add the water, stir well and transfer to the large jar or bottles. Make sure to leave headroom.

For the first couple of days, if using bottles, give them a bit of a tip or shake to get things going, but then put them somewhere safe as they start to come alive. Open after a few days to see if it's working, how it tastes and if it's ready. When it is, put it into the fridge – it won't stop fermenting but it will slow right down.

Notes: *If you'd like to use less whey you can, as this is really just the starter. I use a lot because I like the sour flavour it gives. I like Rivella and they use 35% whey. (From what I can find out, anyway. Their recipe is top secret, you know.)*

I prefer to make this in a large jar with an air-lock because it's easier, but if you don't have a large jar do this in several smaller bottles – it just means you'll have to check on the bottles as they don't let any gases out.

You could easily use water that you've steeped with fruit, tea, herbs, seeds or whatever comes to mind as listed on page 144.

Beet kvass

This is as earthy as it gets! There are many versions of kvass. I'm not a huge fan of the rye one, but that's possibly because I just haven't learnt the right way yet. I'm a fan of beet kvass, although I still have trouble convincing some family members. No worries, I put some into juices and smoothies and everyone is happy – and then there is always fruit kvass. All it needs is a ¼ jar of fruit, 1 teaspoon of honey, a thumb of ginger and water to fill the jar.

This beet kvass recipe is a little unusual because I've added chopped cabbage. This lightens the beet up a bit. Alternatively, you could use sauerkraut juice and leave the cabbage and whey out.

Preparation time: ↓15 minutes
Fermentation time: 5–7 days
Equipment: 5 L (170 fl oz) jar

½ onion
handful of red or green cabbage, chopped
  (optional)
1 tablespoon fennel seeds
2–3 beetroot (beets), peeled and
  roughly chopped
pinch of salt
125 ml (4 fl oz/¼ cup) whey or sauerkraut juice
  (optional)

>>>

BEET KVASS
CROSS-SECTION

BEET KVASS

enough unchlorinated water to fill your jar
(leaving headroom)
small piece of orange zest
couple of slices of fresh ginger

Add the onion, cabbage (if using), fennel seeds, beetroot and salt to your jar and top with the whey (if using) and water, leaving headroom. Seal and leave to sit in a dark place. It should be ready between 5 and 7 days later. Taste it and keep going until you get to the flavour you'd like. Sometimes this only tastes good after refrigeration and a bit more time.

Ginger beer

What better way to fill an 11 year old's need for experimenting and growing something over the holidays? The trick is in keeping the alcohol levels low – about 1.5%. It is still considered a soft drink, so we don't worry too much. We've always measured ours to be under that, and measuring alcohol levels using a cheap hydrometer is another fun sciency thing to do.

I think lots of kids have grown up on ginger beer. This version is a lot better than the sugary shop-bought kind and the satisfaction and pride kids have in making their own brews is high. Many older people have stories of ginger beer and usually talk of the time their ginger beer exploded. We often get 1 or 2 really fizzy bottles that pop and spew and then a few flat ones.

You need to feed this every day, so don't start it the day before going on holiday like Ryder did. He liked it mostly because I think he thought we were going to actually make something with bugs! But as ginger ale is his favourite, he wasn't disappointed at all. The brewing recipe starts you off with small quantities.

Ginger beer bug

Preparation time: ↓15 minutes
Fermentation time: up to 3 weeks
Equipment: small jar, muslin (cheesecloth)

2.5 cm (1 in) piece of fresh ginger (plus an extra 5 pieces for feeding)
2 teaspoons organic sugar (plus extra for feeding)
250 ml (8½ fl oz/1 cup) unchlorinated water

Grate the ginger into a small jar, and add the sugar and water. Cover with a piece of muslin, secure with a rubber band and leave in a warm spot where you won't forget it. Feed it the same amount of ginger and sugar and stir every day. It should start to bubble a bit after a few days. The yeasts and bacteria in there will be enjoying the sugar and ginger and would love to carbonate your ginger beer for you. Keep it alive until the day you want to make the ginger beer (see below).

Brewing ginger beer

Preparation time: 30 minutes
Fermentation time: 3 days–2 weeks
Equipment: muslin (cheesecloth), bottles for storing

4 litres (135 fl oz/16 cups) water
330 g (11½ oz/1½ cups) organic raw (demerara) sugar (see note)
1 thumb-sized piece of fresh ginger (or a whole hand of ginger, depending on how hot you like it), grated but not peeled
juice of about 2 lemons
1 ginger bug (see recipe above)

>>>

GINGER BEER BUG WAITING TO BE FED

Boil 1 litre (34 fl oz/4 cups) of the water and add the sugar, stirring to dissolve, then add the remaining water, ginger and lemon juice.

Line a strainer with muslin and strain your ginger bug, pressing through as much liquid as you can. The remaining pulp can be used to start another mother and will be ready in only a few days.

Add the ginger bug liquid to the sugar mixture and bottle. Leave the bottles in a warm spot for a few days, then taste it. Pop it in the fridge when it's fizzy enough for you. Depending on your ferment, it could take a couple of weeks, but keep an eye on it.

Note: *If you are using glass it's a good idea to bottle one in plastic to see how the ferment is going. When the plastic bottle is tight, it's ready.*

Wild mead

Mead is said to be easy to make, but difficult to make well. True. Maybe. Does 'well' mean delicious enough for your friends to drink it all up after just a few weeks or months of fermenting? Or 'well enough' because smelling and witnessing the alchemy that occurs by simply mixing water and honey together makes your head spin? That happens to me nearly every batch and I am obviously still a beginner. Why would a beginner write about something in an instructional tone? If this encourages you to try it, then that's why. Recipes that have yeasts and racking and all kinds of steps can be daunting and off-putting. This recipe is not that.

Mead should be compared more with a cider than with a beer or wine. I enjoy mead a bit 'green' and young, which is fortunate, as I have trouble saving it. We have people over and next thing you know I am talking about it, showing them and finally of course, offering it around with a warning that it's not all the way perfect. My friends love it and we drink it all up. There, I've done it again. All gone. We don't plan to, but after the first tentative glass you feel as though you want another. No worries, I can make another batch, and maybe this time I'll rack it and save it.

And here's a lovely thing about mead: it is the original honeymoon drink – that's why you'll often see people giving it or providing it at weddings. Historically, the bride and groom were supposed to drink mead every day for the first month of their wedding for fertility! A few glasses of mead is certainly relaxing. A month of mead would be a good way to relax into a marriage ...

Your gateway mead

Differing ratios and honey varieties will produce different outcomes. Plenty of people choose a 1:4 ratio – but mine turns to vinegar quicker if I use that ratio. And not only that – honey is precious. Keep a notebook on what you've used for future experi-ferments.

Mead is the oldest alcohol known. It was probably an accident, a bit of water dripping into a hive and fermenting there. Humans began fermenting and drinking mead before they learnt how to plant seeds or keep animals, so it would be a pity to miss out because this is indeed our most ancient fermented drink.

That's why this is as simple as fermenting gets. I'm pretty happy with a basic, ancient mead like this. If you aren't planning on selling it, or going into competitions with it, then go on and experiment with it. Going deeper into varying meads will reap you some crazy good meads. But this recipe here is your gateway mead.

Preparation time: 5 minutes
Fermentation time: 3 months
Equipment: bucket, crock or large jar, muslin (cheesecloth), narrow-necked bottle, bottles for storing

1 part raw honey
6 parts water (see notes)

Pour the honey and water into an open vessel (a clean bucket or crock or large jar) and stir quite vigorously until the honey and water are one. Cover with muslin or a large tea (dish) towel and label with your recipe, the date and time.

Keep it nearby for the first couple of weeks because you need to stir it. Get hold of a large stick or wooden spoon (or wand, see second column) and stir as often as you think of it. It's important to stir it frequently in those first days. Do it frequently for the first week and less in the second week.

When you stir, try to make a biodynamic-style vortex – stir one way until a whirlpool forms, watch it for a while and then stir it the opposite way. This blends the yeasts into and throughout the honey.

As the froth and bubbles mellow, sometime after week 2, you can start to think about putting it into another vessel – because if you leave it in the open-air vessel, it can turn to vinegar pretty quickly. This is the time to taste and check – don't let it go. There's a fine line here. I aim for a dry, not-too-sweet mead, so I love it as it gets drier and less sweet, but leave it too long and you'll ruin it.

When the bubbling has stopped (or slowed) and it seems the alcohol is reaching a point of decline, then you need to put it into a narrow-necked bottle, preferably with an air-lock.

Wait another couple of months, maybe 3 months, when the activity has slowed all the way, then syphon or pour carefully into bottles without bothering the sediment or lees. I use swing-top bottles for this.

Be warned: open with care, like champagne. Mead can be high in alcohol, and is often very fizzy – I've never had an explosion, but I've had some violent openings. Seriously, this is not for kids.

Notes: *Use rainwater or filtered water, preferably not chlorinated water, and use it at room temperature for the ease of stirring in the honey.*

I use a stick to stir my mead because I've read that the wood allows the yeasts to take hold and live happily within and on the wood, waiting for a chance to come out and inoculate subsequent batches of mead. Birch or any wood that has a sweet sap makes a good stirring stick, or a wand. Soak it in mead, then dry it out, as it will keep the yeast on it as a starter for your next brew. As the wood dries, cracks form, opening the wood up for the yeasts who are still after sugar and will go deeper into the wood and hibernate there for as long as a year.

Understandably in the past the stick was seen as magic because without it the mead didn't take as well. The matriarch traditionally took care of both the brewing and the wand, which was considered sacred and handed down for generations. Oh, to have something magic to hand down to my daughters, and theirs should they have them. My wooden barrels, my wand, my grater. Some bottles of mead?

JUNIPER IS QUITE MAGICAL, YOU KNOW

There is a rye kvass recipe that has juniper as the only flavouring, and the yeast of the dried bread to speed it up. When I read about that, I thought of the simple ferment of just water and juniper berries called *smreka*, which translates directly as juniper – the tree – in Croatian.

Because smreka is made from only two ingredients – juniper berries and water – it's no surprise that the flavour is subtle. I have left it a whole month only to open it up and be a bit disappointed. (I still bottled it, and after adding lemon and sugar, and refrigerating it for a few more days, it became quite refreshing.)

I first read about the healing properties of juniper in *Sacred and Herbal Healing Beers* by Stephen Harrod Buhner. There is an old-fashioned Japanese soda (made from pine

WILD MEAD
BOTTLING

needles) that tastes like the smell of a pine forest. Smreka is similar to that. The flavour is quite boreal and subtle. It's not a drink you'd give to kids, more something you might have in a glass on ice after dinner. If you like gin and the flavour juniper brings to krauts and brines, then you'll enjoy the subtle flavour of smreka.

My Dutch great-step-aunt sipped on a drink every evening that's well known in those parts, called Jenever. She drank it, and encouraged me to also, for 'digestion', much as you would a bitter. Jenever is a Dutch drink that is made from alcohol and juniper berries and is thought to be the mother of gin. Being in the Netherlands, she drank it in little tulip-shaped glasses with teeny tiny spoons to stir the sugar with. It is the nostalgia for her routine – the sigh as she sat down and 'gently' slammed down the glasses and accoutrements to share her tipple – that made me curious to try making smreka.

Smreka

If you have an air-lock use it, as there is sugar and therefore gases that need to get out. I use a Weck tulip jar (nice connection) as you can have the glass lid and switch it over to the glass air-lock lid. Last time I made this I just ended up releasing the gases by opening the lid now and then. Be sure to pick it up and swirl it around every time you pass it.

Preparation time: 5 minutes
Fermentation time: up to 2 months
Equipment: 3 L (100 fl oz) jar with air-lock system

1 cup juniper berries (see notes)
2 litres (68 fl oz/8 cups) water

Put the juniper berries and water into the jar and stir before closing.

Shake the bottle as often as you walk by it. The water quite quickly changes colour to a very light yellow and then a more deep bronze. The berries start to sink to the bottom of the jar. When they are all sitting on the bottom, give it a try, as that's a sign that it's ready. It may take a month or two.

If you don't agitate it often, it may develop a yeasty white film on the top – try to avoid that.

Bottle when ready, chill and drink.

Notes: *Most people won't pick the juniper berries themselves, but if you are lucky enough to be in that position, make sure you look into which is the good kind of juniper berry, and which ones are toxic. Pretty important point. There are a lot of uses for juniper in fermentation – a good one to add to your ferment garden.*

Serve this on ice with sugar and lemon, and as you do, sigh in contentment, and stir it with little spoons.

Switchel

I like an acidic drink at night. Actually, I like wine. But switchel hits the spot as a replacement. When I feel like picking and eating between meals, a large glass of this does the job. Similar to kombucha, it also makes me feel fresher and just happier in general. Maybe I'm one of those people that doesn't drink enough water and switchel makes me want more? (This is the way Ma got Pa to drink more water on hot days out in the field in *Little House on the Prairie*. Big fan. Even spent a winter in a cabin near their original home of Walnut Grove.)

The drink's name sounds adorably hillbilly, but in fact, vinegar drinks have a very long history around the world – from *sekanjabin* in Iran, to *posca* in ancient Greece and Rome and *oxymel* during the Renaissance. Whatever switchel's history, here we are, and it is a thirst-quenching drink, particularly on hot days or when you're doing something pure and healthy, like living a month with no wine in Dry July or Ocsober.

I make it with a splash of vinegar, a quick dash of maple syrup and then water with ice. If it's too vinegary, add more water. That's it. The syrup is for sweetness and doesn't taste of maple at all. I also have a fig syrup that I use sometimes.

Here's a recipe, but feel free to adjust to your taste. Some people are 2 parts vinegar to 1 part maple syrup types, but I have a love of sour. Makes my heart race.

SERVES: 1

1 tablespoon maple syrup (or other sweetener; maple is my favourite for this)
3 tablespoons apple cider (or rice) vinegar
250 ml (8½ fl oz/1 cup) water
ice, to serve

>>> *continued on page 156*

Combine the ingredients in a glass, then add ice (better for flavour and sound).

Note: *You could grate some fresh ginger into this as well, but that is too many steps for me; it tastes fine the way it is.*

Shrub

While switchel is simply made by mixing a sweetener with a vinegar and adding water, a shrub is made from a blend of fruit and sweeteners – like a sweet vinegar cordial.

Shrubs have been around for aeons as well – a popular colonial mixer. A bit more effort is required, but the flavours are more elegant than those of switchel. Keep this in your cupboard at the ready and pour an inch into the bottom of a glass for a refreshing drink. Shrubs are great to mix with an alcohol like gin and sparkling water. Without the gin is fine too, of course, and a good way to feel like you're having a real drink when you're actually not.

The word 'shrub' comes from the Arabic word *sharub*, meaning 'to drink'. This is one possible flavour, but you can work with this recipe to get different styles.

MAKES: 1 LITRE (34 FL OZ/4 CUPS)

100 ml (3½ fl oz) maple syrup, or 100 g (3½ oz) honey or sugar
250 g (9 oz/2 cups) raspberries
130 g (4½ oz/1 cup) blackberries
zest of 1 lemon
2–3 sage leaves, or 1 small rosemary sprig
500 ml (17 fl oz/2 cups) red wine vinegar
500 ml (17 fl oz/2 cups) balsamic vinegar
100 ml (3½ fl oz) water

Simmer the maple syrup, fruit, zest and herbs for 20 minutes in a saucepan over medium heat. Add the vinegars and water and simmer for a further 5 minutes. Strain using muslin (cheesecloth) or a fine sieve, let it cool and then bottle. It will keep in your cupboard for at least 3 months.

Notes: *To drink, add an inch or two to a glass and add either water and ice, or sparkling water. To this, you could also add some bourbon or gin.*

If you wish, you can vary the fruit, and use a different vinegar – try a rice vinegar, or simple white wine vinegar, champagne vinegar, malt vinegar, persimmon vinegar (page 185) or shiso vinegar (page 158).

More on vinegar

In Japanese the 'shi' part of sushi comes from the word for rice – *meshi*. The word *su* in Japanese means sour. So *sushi* means 'soured rice'. Sushi began as a way of preserving fish in between beds of sour, vinegared rice. Initially people only ate the fish, but this later developed into a dish that you ate in its entirety. You can still find a version of this original sushi called *funa zushi*.

What is interesting to me is that at the same time Ma and Pa were drinking vinegared water in Minnesota, and society was enjoying shrubs in England, the Japanese were also imbibing their water with vinegars. Actually Romans were drinking it way before this, and the Okinawans can also trace this back a long way (and they have a famed longevity). Koreans have a history of drinking vinegars as well, and I think we could find the same all over the world.

If you can discover Japanese drinking vinegar in your local specialty shop, try it. It's a touch more refined than apple cider vinegar. I have included a recipe for Persimmon vinegar on

page 185 that you could use for the shrubs, or to make the Shiso vinegar (page 158).

You can also make your own rice vinegar using two parts rice wine and one part water. Pop it into a crock with a vinegar mother, cover as you would kombucha – with a cloth and held with a band – and leave for about a month.

Vinegar mothers work with any liquids – you don't need to buy a certain mother. You can grow one on top of some living vinegar.

Make the surface area equal to the depth – half a jarful, for example. It prefers the dark and a rather warm place if you have one. Check it and when it is sour enough, strain through muslin (cheesecloth) and bottle in a nice sterilised bottle. The longer it sits on your shelf, the more delicious it will be.

Try this with leftover red wine, beer (to get malt vinegar) or champagne.

Shiso vinegar

This isn't a ferment. It's essentially a flavoured vinegar, like a switchel or shrub. If you don't know about the beautiful flavour of shiso (also called perilla leaf) go and find some. It grows very easily and is a fine cross between anise, mint and basil. It complements nattō (page 186), oily meats and sushi, and is used in various Asian dishes. In fact you could add small amounts to any of your ferments as it imparts a gentle flavour. If you use the red leaves (shiso is red or green) the liquid goes bright pink.

For this you need rice or apple cider vinegar. I use rice vinegar (buy a good one if you haven't made your own – see page 157) because the flavour is more delicate, but apple cider vinegar is good too. Shiso vinegar is known to be very healthy, but firstly it is refreshing and delicious.

Preparation time: 30 minutes
Equipment: bottles for storing

about 300 g (10½ oz) red shiso leaves, no stems
2 litres (68 fl oz/8 cups) water
400 ml (13½ fl oz) vinegar (I use rice vinegar)
350 g (12½ oz) sugar

In a saucepan over high heat, bring the leaves and water to a boil. Reduce the heat and simmer for about 5–10 minutes. The water will be bright purple. Cool, then squeeze the leaves out and strain the liquid. Pour the liquid back into the pot, add the sugar and stir to dissolve, then add the vinegar and stir to combine.

Leave to cool and then transfer to clean bottles. Refrigerated, it's good for months.

Note: *Serve in a glass with ice, and perhaps a squeeze of lemon. Add water if it's too astringent for you.*

Fire tonic

It may seem like fire ciders or tonics are following in the kombucha fad direction, but don't be put off by thinking it's a new health fad with no actual depth. This is folk medicine, reviving itself in kitchens all over the world as people from all walks of life try to boost their immunity and keep healthy with natural homemade elixirs. That's a happy thing. If I've left my kombucha too long and it's vinegar I save it and use that vinegar in my fire tonic. That's also a satisfying thing, taking your mistake and levelling up.

Just like other ferments you can certainly, without worry, swap ingredients I've specified for something similar or take them out altogether. I think the main thing is to use quality vinegar. And be sure to wait the whole month.

Preparation time: 20 minutes
Fermentation time: 1 month
Equipment: 5–10 L (170–340 fl oz) tapped vat or jar, muslin (cheesecloth), bottles for storing

3 large pieces of fresh ginger
1 small piece of fresh horseradish, grated
  or chopped (watch out, it will be hot!),
  or 1 tablespoon of the jarred stuff
1 onion, chopped
10 organic garlic cloves, chopped
2 jalapeño chillies, chopped
1 lemon, chopped, or just the zest and juice,
  depending on your jar size
several sprigs of fresh rosemary, chopped
1 tablespoon fresh turmeric, grated,
  or 1 tablespoon ground turmeric
10 cm (4 in) piece of burdock root,
  chopped or grated
1 bunch of parsley, stems only, chopped
1 tablespoon chopped oregano (fresh or dried)

FIRE TONIC
WAITING
FOR ITS
VINEGAR

1 tablespoon black peppercorns
pinch of cayenne pepper
organic apple cider vinegar, or kombucha
    vinegar (I like to use half 'buch vinegar and
    half apple cider vinegar), enough to fill
    your jar
90 g (3 oz/¼ cup) raw local honey, or to taste

Add all the ingredients except the honey to the
jar, adding the vinegar last. Store in a dark, cool
place for about a month, shaking it whenever
you pass it, or once every day or two.

After a month has passed, strain the liquid
into a bowl through some muslin, squeezing
the pulp as you go. Add the honey and stir to
combine. Bottle.
    You don't need to keep this in the fridge.

Note: Small, flask-like bottles are quite hip and
feel edgy to swig from. They are also nice to
surreptitiously give to friends who are coming
down with a cold.

Ferment for good
Drinks

Pineapple wine (pineapple tepache)

This wine is rustic and very basic – we aren't adding yeast. You can add citric acids, tannins and yeasts to help your wine, but you won't read about that in this book. I like the wild aspect – the idea that you aren't going to a specialty shop and buying something to help; that if I were living in a forest a long time ago I would be making it just like this (or well, a tropical island...). For fine wines and beers I rely on people who are focused on that craft, who have attention to detail. I almost idolise them and support them by buying lots of their wares ... I'm so dedicated to this that it sometimes gives me a headache.

The Fermentary started its commercial life in a little building on a beautiful vineyard, so it's fun for me to include a couple of very rugged, country wine recipes – quite the opposite of what was being created there. Everything starts somewhere and gets refined over time, right? This wine is so simple anyone can do it. Why use all of the fruit for jam when you can make wine?

A few important things: first, the younger the wine and the sweeter it is, the less alcohol. If you make a 'wine' with a very sweet fruit it has the potential to reach quite a high alcohol level. Second, this can get pretty fizzy. Like ginger beer or the whey sodas, it makes kombucha and kefir look tame.

When I was in grade 8 at school in Malaysia, we made pineapple wine in science. This was my first introduction to fermentation, but I remember it mainly because we got to bring it home to give to our parents as a present. I was very proud. On the bus on the way home most of the kids sat and drank theirs. I hadn't thought of drinking it myself, luckily, because when my parents opened it the drink fizzed out everywhere. It tasted pretty good though, the little we had left.

Preparation time: 10 minutes
Fermentation time: 4 days
Equipment: 5 L (170 fl oz) jar

2 pineapples, skin on, cut into lengths
230 g (8 oz/1 cup) soft brown sugar
1 tamarind pod, or 1 teaspoon tamarind paste
2 litres (68 fl oz/8 cups) water (some hot, to dissolve the sugar – see notes)
4 cloves (depending on how strong you'd like the flavour)
2 cinnamon sticks

Arrange the pineapple lengths in the jar.

Dissolve the sugar and tamarind paste (if using) into some hot water.

Pour this mixture over the pineapple, add the rest of the water, the cloves and cinnamon, along with the tamarind pod if you didn't use tamarind paste.

Cover with a cloth or paper towel and secure with a rubber band. Keep on your bench at room temperature.

Taste after 4 days and if you're happy with it, strain, bottle the liquid and refrigerate. It will keep in the fridge for at least a few weeks.

Notes: *Coconut water is a great replacement for regular water. Use a little less sugar if you do that.*

The pineapple is still okay to eat after the fermentation time. Alternatively, you could throw it into some water kefir.

As with mead, there's a chance that if you let this go for too long it will turn into vinegar.

Serve over ice with some mint leaves.

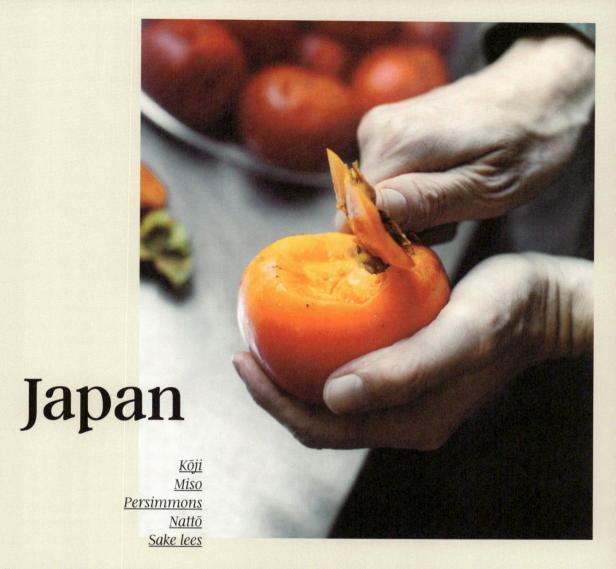

Japan

Kōji
Miso
Persimmons
Nattō
Sake lees

I'm sure you've heard about the impressive lifespan of the Japanese, and I'm confident that their traditional cuisine is why – yes there's green tea, but more than that there's the way their naturally homemade and fermented food is incorporated into most meals. But more recently, along with the rest of the world, they have suffered from palate changes driven by the motto 'faster, bigger, cheaper'. Food manufacturing and food technologists have designed more moveable, shelf-stable foods that are cheaper to produce, package and deliver, but are a far cry from the real thing.

All of our palates have adapted to expect, and sometimes even prefer, these faster, mass-produced copies. Fish sauce for example should include two ingredients only: fish and salt. Add time and the right environment and you see why it should be an expensive item, like a fine wine. Soy sauce should really only contain kōji, soy beans, salt, water and wheat.

There are many other foods that purport to be fermented, but now just include flavour enhancers. If you make your own miso (page 171), you will taste what real tamari tastes like. It's worth making miso for the puddle of tamari liquid atop it alone. And maybe you'll go even further and make your own soy sauce. Homemade soy sauce is deeply rich and complex, and incomparable to the bottled stuff we are all used to.

When I first starting looking into adding kimchi to the range at The Fermentary, and what soy and fish sauces were best to add, I began to feel rather ripped off when I realised what was in the shop-bought stuff. And sad because the taste difference is significant and we are all missing out. I needed my ingredients to be pure and authentic.

As a commercial producer of fermented vegetables and drinks, as small as we are, I know that soy sauce, tamari and the like are difficult to produce and get on shelves in shops – they take time, which is money, and regulations don't like the unpredictable nature of artisan ferments. Too many unknowns! Ancient foods are bound by modern regulations, and science requires us to control the variables. That's why laboratory-produced ingredients such as colours, syrups, preserving agents, thickeners, sweeteners and flavour enhancers have found a home in simple items like soy sauce and fish sauce. And also because it's faster and cheaper to produce that way.

It has taken a lot of time, money and testing trying to prove to our local councils that our methods and procedures – the use of salt and the science of fermentation – is indeed safe. Wild fermentation is safe. No one has ever died from sauerkraut, but I respect that we need to prove this and I appreciate the need to regulate our commercial foods. The shame is that highly processed foods are more readily available than real foods. So it's the small, passionate artisan food producers who will change this. And they are usually also happy to teach people to do it themselves. (Here's to the prospect of many small producers again.) Now, back to Japanese ferments.

This book is designed to draw you in and provide some inspiration and confidence, but not necessarily make you a professional miso maker, for example. I hope you'll become a convert and delve deeper, and play with your own experi-ferments. Or maybe you'll do it just once and choose to buy miso instead, but at least you'll have a deeper understanding of what it is.

But what if you went all the way and entered into your own kōji world? Fresh kōji smells like a newborn baby to me (which I can never get enough of). Some of the ingredients might be out of your way, but it'll be worth it, trust me. Japanese ferments are dear to my heart – Japan is where I first really left home and grew up, learnt to cook, be alone, speak Japanese and ferment stuff.

And I have a deep, dark love of long ferments – they conjure quiet excitement for the future. Just when there's no meal in the day to look forward to (as my head hits the pillow), I remember my soy sauce, miso or fish sauce out in the garage fermenting, curing, ageing. Life is more exciting when you've got a few different ferments brewing ... and sometimes a bit annoying when you know you should have tended to them and haven't. Similar to planting a garden, some things grow quickly and others take years, but we still plant them anyway, and that's how you need to approach fermenting.

Kōji

Kōji is key to many of Japan's traditional foods: miso, soy sauce, sake, mirin, vinegar and ama-zake. When you add it to a variety of foods the magic that results is as wondrous as any wild ferment. It's where you find *umami*. The word 'umami' is a bit overused, but comes from a mix of Japanese words – *umai* which means delicious, and *mi* which means taste. So it means 'delicious taste', but really, it describes the savoury taste that kōji achieves by breaking down proteins into amino acids – including the umami flavour, glutamic acid – and starches into sugars.

Miso and soy sauce are beautiful projects that you can make a lot of and then forget about. A once-a-year project, perhaps, with family and friends, just as the weather starts to cool. Have them join you, make a lot and share it around when it's ready. Any way you do it, you'll need to source some kōji, so let's start with that gorgeous thing – a national treasure in Japan.

A QUICK RUNDOWN ON KŌJI

You may have worked with it already, but if you haven't I'm honoured and excited to be the one to introduce it to you. It can be a bit confusing to start with because the word *kōji* is used to describe the actual fungus – *Aspergillus oryzae* – and then after the fungus is grown on a substrate such as rice, for example, it is also called kōji, this time *kome kōji* (rice kōji). By this, I mean the kōji spores have already inoculated the rice. They can be bought like this, usually dried or frozen. You don't need to grow your own; the recipes here will use pre-prepared rice kōji, which you can get at Japanese and Asian food shops in the fridge or freezer, or online.

As mentioned earlier, the soy sauce you buy is typically pasteurised, as is sake, so the health benefits of kōji are lost. But if you include kōji in miso, soy sauce or ama-zake, or Shio kōji (page 167) as an ingredient in a dressing, for example, you'll get all the benefits from the live enzymes and amino acids.

If you want to make your own kōji, you need to buy the kōji spores, from the fungus *Aspergillus oryzae*. By sprinkling the kōji spores over rice, soy beans or barley and incubating it, you will get rice, barley or soy kōji. You can order the powdered fungus and do this yourself. It requires some patience and three days of humidity and temperature control, but many people do this themselves at home. The instructions come with the spores and they are pretty exacting.

Kōji can also be caught wild, which is exciting. It originally came from a growth on rice – similar to huitlacoche on corn – but can be found growing alongside regular mould on fruit too. But … one thing at a time!

Ama-kōji (sweet kōji)

In Japanese *amai* means sweet, so *ama-kōji* means sweet kōji. It is a fantastic way to sweeten foods without sugars. Marinating salmon in it is delicious (see page 166).

It's crazy that just adding kōji to rice and water can result in such sweetness. It's a lovely thing to sip on a cold morning – nourishing, warm and sweet.

Preparation time: 1 hour
Fermentation time: overnight
Equipment: food-grade thermometer, rice cooker (or slow cooker)

200 g (7 oz) rice (see notes)
200 g (7 oz) rice kōji
200 ml (7 fl oz) water

First, cook the rice according to the packet directions, then cool to at least 60°C (140°F). Crumble in the rice kōji, add the extra 200 ml (7 fl oz) water and stir to combine.

At this stage you want to keep it at a constant temperature of about 60°C (140°F). I achieve that by keeping the rice cooker on the 'warm' setting with the lid ajar, but with a tea (dish) towel over the top. You can also easily do this with a slow cooker set to 60°C (140°F), or with the oven on low. Open it up to give it a stir now and then in the first hour or two. I usually leave it like this overnight and then awake to a beautiful aroma.

It will keep for about a week – heat before eating each time. It may change somewhat and become less sweet as it keeps fermenting, even in the fridge. To keep it stable, and the flavour and enzymes intact, you can store it in the freezer for up to 6 months. Thaw before using.

Notes: *Short-grain rice produces a very sweet drink, and medium-grain less sweet. Combine the two for a happy medium, or make it with all short-grain if you intend to use it as a sweetener in your chai, for example.*

When using it in chai tea, you essentially use the ama-kōji as the milk and sweetener. This is great for the dairy-free person in our home. You can also try it as a kind of ice cream – blend the ama-kōji with 200 ml (7 fl oz) of extra water until smooth, add cocoa powder to taste, then freeze or put into your ice-cream maker.

Ama-kōji cured salmon

<u>SERVES: 2</u>

2 fillets of salmon
salt, to taste
2–3 tablespoons ama-kōji (page 165)

Season the salmon by sprinkling it with salt and let it sit, covered in the fridge, for about 20 minutes.

Rinse gently and then pat dry with paper towel. Cover the fillets with the ama-kōji, then cover and store in the fridge overnight.

Before you grill the fish, wipe as much of the kōji off as you can. Be aware that the sugars have been brought to the surface and may burn easily. Grill to rare or medium-rare, and the salmon will be lovely and buttery.

Ama-zake (sweet sake)

Ama-zake is simply watered down ama-kōji. Traditionally mochi rice is used to make ama-zake because it is high in gluten – but it doesn't matter too much. You can add sake lees (page 190) to this to bring the alcohol up if that's what you are after, but this simple ama-zake is for drinking before the sugars have converted to alcohol. It is a deliciously warming traditional drink and is known to be very nutritious. It's particularly good when you are under the weather a little, served with a touch of grated ginger on top.

To make ama-zake refer to the ama-kōji recipe (see left column) and simply add more water to the rice cooker. You can even blend it to make a smoother drink if you prefer.

....

Shio kōji

Shio means salt, so this is simply salted and soaked rice kōji. It is liquid like a rice porridge. It's great for cooking and pickling with as the enzymes in kōji break proteins into amino acids that get turned into glutamate – the umami factor. You can buy already prepared shio kōji, but it is quite often heat-treated for logistics and shelf life, so its power is completely nullified.

Ferment for good
  Japan

Best to make your own, which is very easy once you have rice kōji.

Preparation time: 5 minutes
Fermentation time: 5+ days
Equipment: 1 L (34 fl oz) jar

200 g (7 oz) prepared rice kōji
50 g (1¾ oz) salt
250 ml (8½ fl oz/1 cup) lukewarm water

Break up the rice kōji and rub until aromatic. Add the salt and water and stir to combine.

Transfer the mixture to the jar, cover with the lid and set aside.

Stir once a day. You may need to add water on the second day if all the water has been absorbed – just add enough to cover.

Depending on the temperature in your kitchen, fermentation could take 5 days to 2 weeks. Taste now and then – it should be sweet and salty with a pleasant smell. It may start off too salty, but fermentation will sweeten it somewhat. When you detect the sweetness, pop the jar into the fridge for use. It will keep for at least 6 months.

Note: *Shio kōji can replace salt or soy sauce – it provides the salt and a little extra. Use about 2 teaspoons of shio kōji for 1 teaspoon of salt. For example, mix about 2 teaspoons of shio kōji with 1 mashed avocado instead of salt and the colour will keep.*

Shio kōji pickles

Shio kōji is an easy vehicle for quick pickles. I've left carrots in there for a long time and when I've pulled them out they glowed bright orange, which is freaky really because it's all natural! This makes them pretty spectacular, and you'll feel like telling everyone 'look how orange this is – its natural!' Well, maybe they won't appreciate it as much as you do, and they may take a bite and just say that it's kind of sour. Or they might go crazy for it.

Eating a few pieces of this with a cup of green tea while working at my computer is a happy thing for me. Not as happy perhaps as working with a glass of wine and olives, but you can't do that all of the time … not really.

The golden ratio with shio kōji for any vegetable is 1:10 – this is the general rule, but in saying this I just use whatever I need to cover the vegetables, keeping in mind it's quite salty.

Preparation time: 5 minutes
Fermentation time: 20 minutes, to 1+ days
Equipment: zip-lock bag or shallow dish with lid

carrots, Lebanese (short) cucumbers or green beans
enough shio kōji to cover your vegetables

Prepare the vegetables: peel and chop the carrots into angular pieces; slice the cucumbers into diagonal pieces; blanch the green beans.

Fill a zip-lock bag or shallow dish with enough shio kōji mixture to cover the amount of vegetables you have. Slide the vegetables in there, making sure to coat them completely. (I like to use a zip-lock bag because it uses less shio kōji and I can kind of massage them a bit.) Transfer to the fridge.

The carrot can remain in the fridge overnight or for a few days – longer if you like. The cucumber will be quite quick (20 minutes or so) and the green beans will take a couple of hours.

Rinse the shio kōji off before eating.

Notes: *You can pretty up the carrots by adding a dash of sesame oil and a sprinkling of sesame seeds.*

While the green beans are marinating, mix some shio kōji with black sesame seeds and a sprinkle of chilli flakes, to taste. When your beans are ready, rinse, choose a nice plate, pour the dressing over and mix. Yum.

Shio kōji fried chicken (karaage)

Using shio kōji to marinate your meat may be the best idea in this book. Chicken pieces turn tender and delectable, with a veal-like texture. This is not just for deep-fried pieces; you can add shio kōji to any meat marinade. This is another family favourite.

SERVES: 4

4 tablespoons shio kōji
1 teaspoon grated fresh ginger
1 teaspoon crushed or grated garlic
1 teaspoon soy sauce
450 g (1 lb) boneless chicken thighs, with skin, cut into 2.5 cm (1 in) pieces
60 g (2 oz/½ cup) potato flour or cornflour (cornstarch)
vegetable or canola oil, for deep-frying
lemon wedges, to serve

Combine the shio kōji, ginger, garlic and soy sauce and pour over the chicken. Cover and place in the fridge to marinate for a few hours or a couple of days.

Heat the oil for deep-frying to about 170°C (340°F).

Put the potato flour in a plastic bag, add the chicken pieces and shake to coat.

Gently add the chicken to the oil and fry until golden – don't put too many in at once. Drain on paper towel and serve with lemon wedges. Yummy.

Shio kōji lettuce salad

This is a great way to eat iceberg lettuce; our kids love it.

SERVES: 5

1 tablespoon shio kōji
2 tablespoons vinegar (rice, shiso or a sweeter one like plum or persimmon, for example)
2 tablespoons sesame oil
1 iceberg lettuce, washed and pulled into bite-sized pieces
2 sheets dried nori, or 2 tablespoons dulse flakes

Mix the shio kōji, vinegar and sesame oil together and coat the lettuce with the mixture. Tear the nori or cut it with scissors into small pieces (kids love doing this) and mix this through too. Simple, very refreshing and, shhh, pretty good for the gut.

Note: *You could also use the combination of oil, vinegar and shio kōji as a dipping sauce for cooked soba noodles, or toss through roasted beetroot (beets).*

Miso

Making your own miso may seem quite a process, but it's rewarding, and the liquid that sits on top contains so much umami you'll hit the wall with happy mouth. Don't be put off by the time involved. Growing a vegetable takes a season. People aren't put off from growing an apple tree because it'll be a few years until they get an apple, are they? Think of your ferments in the same way: plant now, benefit later. Ideally you'd make your miso in cooler weather, in late autumn (fall), and then it will go through a cool winter, easing into a warm summer. You can wait a year, right?

The hardest part about making miso is getting kōji for the first time. (See page 165 for more on sourcing kōji.) Once you have the kōji, all you need is salt and beans or legumes to make your own miso. And time of course. But the complexities of miso can go further – the soil the beans were grown on, the substrate the kōji was grown on, the way the beans were prepared, the length of fermentation, the kind and amount of salt. Miso has its own 'terroir'. Traditionally, miso is barley, rice or soy, but you can use hemp, adzuki beans, chickpeas, buckwheat or corn – it really is just a matter of fine balance.

In most parts of Japan they only use rice – that's the most popular – but in other areas they use a mixture of barley, soy and rice. There's red miso that is the oldest and strongest, often three years old; then there are the shorter and less salty misos – the sweet white miso is only fermented for a few months and is lovely on corn or potatoes, as well as in ramen broth or soup.

The ratio is one part beans to one part kōji. You can use a variety of beans mixed with the soy or instead of soy.

Ferment for good
Japan

Miso

Preparation time: overnight + 1 day
Fermentation time: 6–12 months
Equipment: crock, weight

1 kg (2 lb 3 oz) organic soy beans
1 kg (2 lb 3 oz) rice kōji
400 g (14 oz) fine sea salt, plus extra, for sprinkling
1 tablespoon existing miso (unpasteurised if possible)

Soak the soy beans overnight; drain. Transfer to a saucepan, cover with water, place over high heat and bring to a boil. Lower the heat and simmer until a bean can be squeezed easily with your thumb and little finger. This can take a few hours. Save 300 ml of the cooking water.

When the beans are ready, mash them into a paste. I don't like it too smooth, so I leave some beans uncrushed here and there.

Meanwhile, mix the rice kōji with 200 ml of the lukewarm cooking water and the salt. Add the salted rice kōji and the existing miso to the beans and mix well. I use my hands for this.

After mixing well, roll the paste into balls and throw them into your crock, pushing down to get all air pockets out as you go. If the mix seems too dry (if it cracks), add a little more of the cooking water. The mix should be smooth. Some people use beautiful washi paper to top the miso with. We just sprinkle salt over the top and use another bag full of salt as a weight, or some plastic wrap and a couple of rocks.

Date your jar and note the ingredients. Even though you think you'll remember what you've

MISO AGED FOR 10 MONTHS

done, you won't – it's a year's wait and you will forget. Write about it, put it away and try to forget it. Pretty exciting, right?

Notes: *To get a sweet white miso, use more rice kōji than soy beans, 15–20% less salt and ferment for 3–6 months.*

Ferment for good
Japan

Tamari traditionally came from the surface liquid formed during the miso making process. I believe it is worth making miso for this flavour alone. Real tamari is so deep, flavourful, and rich that you can't compare it with what's readily available today.

Miso soup

You could easily replace your morning coffee with a cup of miso soup – or if that's too radical then have it for your morning tea. It is so uplifting. A bowl of this with simple cooked rice, and some pickles or nattō, is a very refined meal indeed.

SERVES: 4

1 litre (34 fl oz/4 cups) water
5–10 cm (2–4 in) piece of kombu (see notes)
1 cup loosely packed bonito flakes (katsuobushi)
2 dried shiitake mushrooms, sliced or whole
handful of chopped greens
250 g (9 oz) tofu, chopped
2 cm (¾ in) piece of fresh ginger, grated
3–4 tablespoons miso
30 g (1 oz/½ cup) chopped spring onions (scallions)

In a saucepan over medium heat, simmer the water, kombu and bonito flakes for 10 minutes, then reduce the heat to low and cook for a further 5 minutes. Strain, pour the liquid back into the saucepan and place over low heat.

Add the mushrooms, greens, tofu and ginger, then add the miso just before serving (see notes). Sprinkle the spring onion on top, to serve.

Notes: *You can keep the wet, cooked kombu and while it's still warm, make a quick pickle to add to rice (see page 175).*

It's best to take out a bit of the stock and stir in the miso to make sure you have blended it all through. You can buy a small strainer that sits in the pot that you add the miso to and it gets blended in that way. I still have mine from my days in Tokyo. I have used it again and again in many different ways.

No boiling the soup after the miso is added. While you want it nice and warm, the enzymes won't stand up to heat over about 70°C (158°F).

I like to keep it simple, but you can make it quite rich by adding heartier things like diced pumpkin or even finely sliced pork, making it into tonjiru *– a pork miso stew.*

Miso dama

These are convenient and portable little balls of health and happiness. Roll them up and add to a thermos for school, have for a quick breakfast or keep them in the fridge at work for a quickie warm up any time.

This recipe is just a guide – add whatever flavours you like. We love fresh grated ginger in our miso, it's calming and refreshing. Our favourite combination is below, for more inspiration check the notes. The key is to chop everything quite finely so it fits into the balls nicely. Feel free to add more substantial ingredients when you dissolve the balls in water.

MAKES: 6–8 BALLS

2 g cut dried wakame, finely chopped
2–5 g bonito flakes (katsuobushi)
200 g (7 oz) miso paste
2.5–7.5 cm (1–3 in) piece of ginger, washed but not peeled, finely grated
2 large dried shiitake, finely diced
5 cm (2 in) block deep fried tofu, tofu skins, or tofu pockets, finely chopped
1 spring onion (scallion), very finely diced
sesame oil, for rolling

In a bowl, mix all the ingredients to form a paste. Take a tablespoon of mixture and roll into a ball. Repeat until all the mixture is used. Wet your hands or use sesame oil to keep the balls from sticking – the oil adds a bit of flavour at the same time.

To store, layer the balls in an airtight container, or wrap them in a small square of

MISO DAMA
FILLINGS

wax paper or plastic wrap, twist the end, and pack into a jar. To drink, cover a ball with 200 ml (7 fl oz) boiling water in a mug or bowl.

Notes: *I have tried plenty of elaborate combinations, but the simplest are the best every time. You can use good quality powdered dashi, small dried fish, 1–2 tablespoons of black sesame paste, dried daikon (3–5 pieces depending on size, finely chopped) or even 1–2 tablespoons of kimchi paste. This makes a lovely spicy soup reminiscent of Thai tom yum.*

Ferment for good
<u>Japan</u>

Kombu pickle

Keep the kombu from the Miso soup (page 174) to make this pickle, which is a good rice topping.

7 cm (2¾ in) piece of kombu, wet from cooking, rinsed and chopped into small pieces
4 tablespoons soy sauce
1 tablespoon mirin
1 tablespoon sake (see note)
1 teaspoon toasted sesame seeds
3–4 teaspoons bonito flakes (katsuobushi)

In a saucepan over medium heat, simmer the kombu, soy sauce, mirin, sake and sesame seeds until glossy. Take off the heat, add the bonito flakes and stir to combine. Pop into a jar, then into your fridge for later.

Note: *A lot of Japanese cooking requires sake. In the case of sake (unlike wine), cheaper is better for cooking. Refined, delicate sake is lower in umami-enhancing compounds, so don't go buying the most expensive stuff just for cooking.*

Misozuke – a miso bed for fermenting in

Miso also makes a great bed to ferment vegetables in, or to cure them to keep for later. It gives them a lovely sheen and gentle sourness. This is one of the easiest ways to preserve vegetables. Like shoving them back into the soil, you plant them in and eat them when you like.

Preparation time: ↓10 minutes
Fermentation time: varies with the vegetable

1 cup miso paste
2 tablespoons mirin
2 tablespoons sake
1 teaspoon salt

Mix the ingredients together and put in a large glass container, or food-grade plastic container with a lid. If you take care of this paste by straining it if it gets too watery, then you may have it for 10 or more uses. Continue using it until it gets too watery.

Notes: *If you want to put watery vegetables in the misozuke, toss them in salt for a while, then drain and rinse before adding them.*

Good vegetables include carrots, daikon (white radish) and little turnips. Peel and chop into large pieces. When you put them in the miso bed, make sure they are completely covered, and depending on the kind of vegetable, leave them for anywhere between 30 minutes and a day. You can leave garlic in there for much longer, and burdock root too – for years.

If you'd like to use garlic, peel the cloves and boil for a few minutes. Pop into the miso, and leave for a couple of weeks. Pull them out as you'd like to eat them, scraping the miso off to your taste. They get better over time. And when you're done, the miso makes a delicious soup.

Egg yolks cure beautifully simply in miso without the other ingredients. Make a little yolk-sized indentation in some miso paste and layer a thin piece of muslin (cheesecloth) over the top. Gently put the yolk on top. Follow with a layer of muslin and then cover with miso. Cover with plastic wrap and put in the fridge. Leave for about 5 days and then gently check. They should be a little see-through and sliceable. You can wrap them in muslin and hang to cure further to make them grateable. I've left mine in the fridge for a few weeks with almost the same result. But hanging little yolks in muslin is lovely. Grate them over anything that needs a little savoury creamy hit. The most common way I enjoy them is in place of parmesan cheese, or in a furikake mix to coat rice balls in a bento box.

After living with a Japanese family as a nanny in inner Tokyo for a year, I took off to a smaller town where I could afford the rent, to immerse myself in a different side of Japan. Reflecting back I sometimes wonder why I was so strict with myself, why I didn't just live with a bunch of friends and have more fun. But I spent a good five years living at the base of Mount Takao, working at a girl's university high school. Originally, I got that job as a personal assistant to the head of the English department, but three months in he passed away and I became the new head, which is why I stayed so long. It was right on the edge of outer Tokyo; the very next stop after Takao station is no longer even Tokyo. It was a gorgeous village that people travelled to for day trips, to climb Mount Takao (*Takao-san*) and to visit the temple on the top of the mountain. I was in a bigger apartment than most of my inner city friends – still rabbit warren-esque but large enough to hold a tatami room that held a *kotatsu* (see below) and another bedroom. Luxury.

A *kotatsu* is a table that's underside is a heater. The tabletop comes off and a large quilt goes on, then the table top is replaced. You all sit there at the table with your legs underneath, quilt over your lap, all cosy and warm (often eating mandarins and rice crackers and watching crazy TV). We need those here!

When I first moved to Takao, I was 24 and the only foreign woman in town, and probably the only six-foot person. My boyfriend moved in with me, and our first and only friends for a couple of years were all over 65. First off, we met the volunteer fire brigade by walking by one of their raucous 'meetings' one Sunday afternoon. I think half of them were functioning alcoholics and thank god there were no fires in our little town. They adopted us like mascots, found any excuse for a drink or ten, even

hosted a huge welcome party when my parents visited. They also quickly invited my American boyfriend to join their baseball team, which soon fizzled out when their dream of an 'import' went sour. He was from a Minnesotan dairy farm and had never really played much baseball. We had tried to warn them but they wouldn't believe us, thinking we were being humble or something. The whole thing was indeed quite humbling for my boyfriend and memorable for me – their uniform was teeny tiny.

More importantly (and this is why I'm glad I moved to Takao and didn't stay in town closer to my other expat friends), I made friends with a gentle old lady who had a lovely little garden just down from my apartment. I used to watch her from my very tiny balcony when I was hanging clothes to dry on my dinky plastic peg thingy. I tried to take some sneaky photos of her, and she eventually waved for me to come down and join her. She was quite ancient, always smiling and hunched over. Her vegetable garden was gorgeous, right below a temple and tucked into the side of the hill, and in spring it was shadowed by overhanging cherry blossoms. She spent her time weeding and picking and would hand lots of vegies to me from her position, almost always squatting. I am so bad at the squat, and much to her disapproval and amusement I usually got my knees very dirty helping her.

I had no idea what to do with some of the vegetables she gave me. I had joined a club that delivered exactly the right ingredients and the recipe direct to my door and didn't need extra food, but never mind. (Yes, that style of club existed in Japan over 20 years ago, called 'dinner service' for the poor souls who worked and had no one home to cook for them. On reflection, it was such a great teacher of technique, home cooking and Japanese food terminology.)

It was this *obasan* who showed me through often impatient sign language what to do with the vegetables we'd picked, and later how to make miso, a nuka bed, how to shove the vegies into the miso to preserve them or enhance the flavour, and how to salt freshly picked cherry blossoms to eat later. I'm sure her family thought it hilarious that she was brave enough to come into my home and hang out with me. I never even met them. Maybe she lived alone.

I also had a kind of funny relationship with the restaurant owner and chef down the road. If I'm honest, he probably started out feeding me so that I could give his country restaurant an international flair – as though I were Brooke Shields (that's who I was always compared to … also 'Lady Diana' as they called her … surely only because of my height because we really bear no resemblance). Months went by and I was calling him Otosan – Dad. We had adopted each other and knew where we stood. Feed me, and I'll sing karaoke later. If he ever had dignitaries coming or someone special we'd be put into the front room where they were sure to walk by, and later even asked to join them for dinner (my boyfriend too!) like some weird entertainment. In return I felt safe and at home in the neighbourhood. He was a highly qualified sashimi chef and his restaurant quite famous. It had one of those floors with water and fish swimming through it. You stepped across stones to get to your individual tatami room to eat. It was here that I had the most wonderful education in all of the foods my meagre teacher's salary would never have afforded me. He fed us puffer fish over and over again, and all of the craziest living (quite cruel) versions of sashimi there were. When my family visited we went together, squashed in the seats of his truck, which carried a tank full of water, window and all, like an aquarium. He'd go to the fish market and fill that tank up to take the fish and other crustaceans back to his own restaurant's aquariums for fresh keeping.

He took us to the beach where he dove into the sea again and again for what seemed like way too long each time. We would hold our breath until he finally surfaced with a bag full of sea urchins and other squiggly things hiding in their shells. He took a knife directly to those and sliced or pulled them from their safe homes, his own body still dripping with water. We couldn't refuse to eat it, even if it was only seven in the morning and the only drink was whiskey. (I'd told him that was my dad's favourite drink.)

When I finally made friends my own age, they told me my home looked a bit like a grandma's house – all of the old crocks and things I had. They would tell me that I could easily buy all of my pickles from the convenience shop down the road, or that I could go to Ikea for furniture – no need for the old heavy dark chests I'd started to adore, or the old kimono I had hanging up to help insulate the thin-walled place.

At the time, I felt like I was wasting time, I wasn't moving 'forward'. I would fret that I should move on – back to reality. I eventually did move back to Australia, only to return with two children three years later. On reflection, it was a very important time, not wasted at all. Spending so much time alone, even when in a crowd of people, was probably my most important inner-strength building period. And I learned many vital life lessons, like bento box appreciation, and the importance of a good, hot, deep bath, and singing for stress relief.

When I had decided I needed to heal Lulu's gut with food, it was miso soup, nattō and pickles that were my first and absolute comfort food for her. I leaned heavily on those foods while I learnt ways to fill her with things other than milk kefir. Life is crazy.

Persimmons

Let's talk about the 'Sharon fruit'. I am a huge fan and not because they are my namesake. They have such a lovely woody flavour, not too sweet, and are great for savoury and sweet dishes. I first came to love persimmons in Japan when I was living there. We got boxes of them sent to the house. I hadn't eaten one before, so learnt of them first as *kaki* – their Japanese name. I had to peel them for the first time in front of the whole family – the little boy I babysat had asked me to do it. We were all sitting at the breakfast table and I pretended I knew how; the father watched painfully as I massacred it, before teaching me a more elegant way. That same little boy also got me to peel his grapes and remove the pith from his mandarins – lucky he was cute.

Persimmons all seem to ripen at the same time, and unlike harder fruit like quince and apples, they don't sit and wait very patiently. There are so many rituals and traditions around food preparation and preservation in Japan, but the sight of hanging *kaki* (making them *hoshigaki*) is striking and very memorable. Slow Food USA has put *hoshigaki* in its 'Ark of Taste' – a catalogue of delicious food in danger of extinction. So I thought we'd better hop to it and save them. Last autumn (fall) I made quite a lot at The Fermentary so we could use them in a special water kefir and mead later on.

Turns out that this is a lot of work – a complete labour of love. It's a tinkering, nurturing wait that gives you jelly-like sweet dried fruit for the whole year. The Chinese method is a lot simpler – rather than hanging individually, you lay them out on sheets of wire so the air and the sun can get to them.

To dry them the Japanese way, into *hoshigaki*, it's preferable to pick them with the stem long because you'll want to use that for tying the string. (We have been using whatever persimmons are available, but in Japan there is a longer kind called Hachiya persimmons that are preferable mainly due to their shape.) You'll first need to peel them, then tie a string from the stem and hang them individually from a drying rack, pole or roof. If they have the stem on them you can stick this through the rope thread, which is much easier.

Ideally you would hang these from under the eaves or porch – or put the drying rack somewhere there is sun and a breeze. After about a week they should have shrivelled and you can put them in the shade. You'll need to massage them gently every day though – yes. Do this to help keep the mould at bay and also to distribute the fruit as it softens. After about a month of this they will be dark and soft and you can pull them from the stem and put them in an airtight container to use for the rest of the year. Eat them with a cup of green tea, or chop them and put into a meal or in your kimchi.

(Or skip the ceremony, labour and wait by slicing fresh firm persimmons with a mandoline and drying them in a dehydrator.)

I love fresh persimmons, sliced thin using a mandoline, served on a thin cracker with some goat's curd and a touch of black pepper.

PERSIMMON VINEGAR MOTHER

Kaki-su (persimmon vinegar & a persimmon fermenting bed)

Another great way to use up your persimmons is to make them into vinegar, which is *far* easier than drying them. After you've made vinegar you'll have a bed of persimmons (the pressed fruit – the lees) to ferment other vegetables in. This is a great fermenting bed and can also replace *umeboshi* (dried plums) in dressings. It is largely a Korean vinegar, but I also saw it in Nancy Singleton Hachisu's book where she introduced me to the idea of using the lees for fermenting.

Preparation time: 20 minutes
Fermentation time: 3 months
Equipment: large jar, muslin (cheesecloth), bottles for storing

10 or more persimmons

Take the top off each persimmon – the calyx – by going in with your knife to cut around it.

Stack them gently in a large jar top-side down and cover with a secured cloth.

About a week later they should be soft and gel-like inside. This will depend on the temperature in your house of course – it could take a bit longer. When they are all gel-like, take them out and trim off any mould. (Eat one now if you like – SO delicious.)

Put them back into the vessel top-side down, and squish each one down firmly. (This is fun.) You should end up with a smooshy-looking stack.

Cover with a secured cloth for more waiting.

Within a few days there'll be a clear liquid at the bottom and the fruit will have softened into more of a paste. At this stage, you'll need to stir well every couple of days, mixing in the yeast that forms on top and keeping it blended. When your mixture has a vinegar smell, which won't take long, let it sit without stirring.

Because you are using an autumn (fall) fruit, your house won't be warm, which is good for a slow ferment. After about 3 months, before it gets too warm, line a fine strainer with muslin and sit it over a bowl. Slop the fruit into the muslin and let it seep through into the bowl. After a few hours, cover the fruit with the muslin corners and add a weight to get as much liquid as possible from it. When you think it's all out, squeeze the muslin bag to get more. (Store the mash for later use; see below.)

Bottle the liquid up and store to use as a concentrate for drinking vinegar, or on salads or in dressings.

Notes: *Don't wash the fruit too well – the white film you may see on the peel is what will help it ferment. This is thought to be very good for the liver. Drink it as a shrub with a dash of honey and some water.*

To ferment in the persimmon bed

The fruit you'll have left over can be thrown out or into the compost, but you could also keep a jar of it to add to dressings. You can also use it to quick-ferment with by sticking air-dried daikon (white radish), raw turnips or carrots into the bed for a few days to ferment. I've only ever done daikon and cucumber in this – but it's worth trying if you've made the vinegar and have the lees already, right? Just hang out the whole daikon to dry for a few days – until they can be bent. Cut into quarter lengths, stuff into the persimmon bed and cover for a few days. Pull them out and slice into half moons, leaving some of the fruit on them. Cucumbers should be salted first, rinsed and then popped in whole. You can also add this to dressing or sushi.

Nattō

When I first moved to Japan, I was 23, and my first job was at a ski resort working in the restaurant at the very top of the mountain. Skiing home at night, and all through my lunch hour, I thought I'd hit the jackpot. We wore a cartoon-esque outfit of khaki safari shorts with pink and white striped button-up shirts and pink bow ties, with long white socks. My uniform was on the small side, of course. I stood behind a bain-marie serving curry, katsu-curry or hashed beef with a plonk of ginger pickle. My portions were so generous I kept getting in trouble from the owner. We counted the hours until we could either eat the curry ourselves or have a break and a bit of a ski ... until I had a little accident, which put me out of skis and into the ski rental at the bottom of the mountain and in a shop with the oldest men I'd ever met.

The quiet period at that ski rental place was just about all day – there was a hectic hour in the morning, and a busy period late in the afternoon as they all returned their equipment. In the quiet time in between we sat around and stared into space. I made the others tea and practiced writing various words in Japanese. We sat around a kerosene heater with a special plate on top that hosted a continuously boiling kettle. In the late afternoon we heated up dried squid, and they would yell my name (after discussing with each other semi-quietly how to say my name again) and ask for *ochazuke*. Make tea. That's how I started to learn Japanese. I could effortlessly ask people their personal information for the rental form and their sizes, but had trouble writing down their answers, and would always hand it over for them to fill out themselves. They could have written anything.

In the dormitory we stayed in, most mornings breakfast was nattō and miso soup, sometimes fish, always raw eggs if you wanted, and of course rice. It took about a month to get used to the nattō, but after that and ever since then I crave it. It's like blue cheese I guess ... some people don't like the ammonia-like smell, or the texture, but once you get used to it you usually start to love it. Even if you don't love it you can add nattō to pancakes or stir-fries or just a bowl of rice, and it's particularly delicious in sushi, mixed first with some light soy sauce and laid over a shiso leaf.

The nattō bacteria are powerful and very good for you. They're so powerful that people who work in sake factories aren't allowed to eat nattō: one little bit of nattō culture and the whole sake batch could be ruined. Imagine how powerful it would be to a parasite or toxins in your gut. With the amount of raw fish they eat in Japan, perhaps their love of nattō isn't purely a happy coincidence.

Nattō is simply soaked and cooked soy beans, a culture, the right temperature and time. More patience than work, as each stage takes time and care.

If you feed it to your children early on they will love it. The flavour is kind of yeasty or like fragrant ammonia – not very bad; it's more the texture that could be off-putting. The beans are bound together somewhat with a viscous stringiness that people don't love at first sight. But I feel that it was a key part of Lulu's gut healing journey. Watching your child enjoy a bowl of miso and nattō with rice for breakfast before school feels good.

Nattō can be made by back-slopping – you take some existing nattō and add it to soy beans to make another batch of nattō. Or if you are up for it, try getting the culture wild. But it can be done by rubbing the cooked beans with fresh fig or even fern leaves. The yeast on the leaves has a similar kind of yeast as the nattō culture. The traditional way to make it is by putting the warm beans into a wad of straw.

Whenever a starter culture is called for, I always wonder where it came from originally, or how it has been grown and made. But for nattō the way I make it at the moment is with the nattō culture from Japan. Nattō and kōji starter powders are the only manufactured starter cultures we use at The Fermentary.

So, to making nattō: be sure to keep everything clean, as usual. If you are using spores, they come with instructions and their own little spoon, which you should be sure to use and treasure forever, because it's TINY. The nattō needs to incubate at around 40°C

(105°F) for 24 hours. I use my oven at its lowest temperature, but using an electric blanket or heat pad works too.

Aim to eat your fresh nattō for breakfast by starting the process on this timeline: soak overnight, cook all the next day, incubate all night, then refrigerate. Maybe start Friday night for a Monday breakfast or lunch, for example.

Nattō

Preparation time: a few days
Fermentation time: 24 hours
Equipment: 3–4 glass baking dishes, or something similar that is shallow and large and has a fitted lid, sterilised (by boiling in water for about 10 minutes), muslin (cheesecloth)

740 g (1 lb 10 oz/4 cups) dry soy beans
2 teaspoons boiled and cooled water
1 tiny little spoon of nattō powder (or
   1 teaspoon of actual nattō)
soy sauce, to taste
English mustard, to taste

Rinse, then soak the beans overnight using plenty of water, because they expand. You will end up with 8–12 cups of beans.

Drain the beans and simmer steadily in a saucepan over medium heat, adding water as needed. It's best to cook them for about 9 hours. Yes.

Drain the beans and transfer to a clean saucepan.

In a small bowl, mix the nattō powder with the water.

Pour the nattō spore solution over the beans while they are still warm. Gently stir to combine and inoculate.

Carefully spread a thin layer of beans into each dish – if you drop a bean here and there, leave it out, as we don't want any contamination.

Place the muslin over the top of the beans, then cover with aluminium foil with a few holes punched through.

Place in an incubator – an oven at about 40°C (105°F) for 24 hours. You need a high-humidity environment for nattō – so a dish of water in the oven will help too.

Let the nattō cool for a couple of hours, then remove the lid and cloth. Replace the lid and leave in the fridge for another 24 hours or overnight. The taste will mature over the course of a week, so if you are planning to freeze it, wait the week out first. Pack it into smaller portions to freeze and pull out as needed. Nattō does very well frozen, and is often sold that way.

To eat, stir in soy sauce to taste, and a touch of English mustard – just a touch at a time. Stir vigorously to make the nattō all foamy.

Notes: *Serve over rice with a bowl of miso soup for the best breakfast ever.*

Add some nattō and a shiso leaf to sushi, or on its own to okonomiyaki, steamed vegetables or salads.

STRINGY NATTO

Sake lees

I'm pretty excited to be writing about sake lees right now. Initially I was worried that you wouldn't be able to get your hands on any and didn't want to tease you with this. But sake lees is experiencing a true renaissance in Japan, where it has long been easily available in the fresh food section of any grocer. It is also widely available in parts of the US. Just like a SCOBY this is something you may or may not need to search for.

Sake lees is a by-product in the sake (rice wine) making process, and has been used for flavour and cooking in Japan for a very long time. Sake lees will add a certain *umami* when used with other products, or can be used as a vehicle for further fermentation. Fresh sake smells pretty yeasty, like beer or brewer's yeast. You may get it in sheet form, or the softer, hand-pressed kind. I can get the softer variety frozen and imported from our Japanese food shop, but the sheet style comes from a sake brewery just outside of Sydney. Sheet form is probably more common, but has been pressed by machinery rather than hand squeezed. The hand-pressed kind is called *namakasu* (raw lees).

Sake lees is a great marinade (see page 192) – blend it with soy sauce, honey and a herb, such as thyme, and use as a marinade for duck, chicken or a dense fish such as mackerel. We've done this quite a bit with chicken pieces before putting them onto skewers. Leave coated in this marinade, covered and refrigerated for a full 24 hours. The flavours are deep and the meat tender.

Sake lees pickle bed (sake kasu)

It's not pretty, but I use a zip-lock bag and it sits on the top shelf in the fridge door, so I can easily give it a bit of a massage and a feel when I remember.

Preparation time: 15 minutes
Fermentation time: 4–5 days
Equipment: zip-lock bag or small bowl with a lid or pickle press or jar

50 g (1¾ oz) sake lees, torn into small pieces
3 tablespoons water
2 tablespoons sugar
2 teaspoons salt
herbs and spices, to your liking (optional; see notes)
carrots or burdock, washed, peeled and cut into rectangular slices (see notes)

In a bowl, combine the sake lees and water. Massage the lees vigorously until you get a paste. Add the sugar, salt and herbs and spices (if using), then mix well to a thick consistency.

Pour the lees mixture into a plastic zip-lock bag, small bowl with a lid, pickle press or jar.

Add the carrot or burdock slices and massage through well, so that the vegetables are coated in the sake lees mixture.

Leave to marinate in the fridge.

In 4–5 days, the vegetables will have become delicious lees pickles. Wipe off the excess sake lees and serve.

MASSAGING SAKE LEES WITH YUKO

Notes: The sake lees pickling bed can be reused 2–3 more times. When you're finished with it, pop it into your compost, chook food or pet food, a bit at a time.

You can add chilli or herbs and spices to flavour the sake kasu.

You can also use other vegetables. For daikon (white radish), regular radish or cucumbers and other watery vegies, sprinkle with a little salt, let rest, then squeeze the water out before adding to the pickling bed. They'll be ready within 24 hours.

Ferment for good
Japan

Sake lees marinated fish

This is a traditional marinade for fish.

SERVES: 4

500 g (1 lb 2 oz) flathead, salmon, mackerel
    or other fish

MARINADE
180 g (6½ oz) sake lees
250 ml (8½ fl oz/1 cup) water, plus enough
    water to make the lees into a paste
2 tablespoons mirin
2 teaspoons soy sauce
pinch of white pepper
5 tablespoons sugar
2 teaspoons salt
2 teaspoons grated fresh ginger

To make the marinade, massage the lees with
a little water until it forms a paste, then slowly
incorporate the remaining ingredients.

Coat the fish in the lees mixture, cover and
leave in the fridge for at least a day.

Wipe the paste off and grill the fish as you
would normally. This is particularly lovely over
a coal barbecue.

You probably know that Japanese food is
delicate and refined but humble. Traditional
foods are mostly rice, vegetables, seafood, fowl
and eggs, but never dairy and rarely beef.

Before World War II, when the arrival of
foreigners to Japan was less common, the smell
of a foreigner was so pungent to Japanese
people, who were unused to meat fats and dairy,
that they said an American's or European's skin
smelt quite sour, like butter. In fact, the rude
term for a foreigner was once *bata kusai*, which
means 'butter stinker'. This was also because
the Japanese evening bath rituals were so
sophisticated compared to those of the rugged
and ship-weary foreigners.

Can you truly smell dairy on a person
through their skin? I used to wonder about that
on my commute in crowded trains in Japan. Did
I smell? I loved Japanese-style bathing so much
and ate a Japanese diet. But I also loved butter
and cream. Was dairy pouring out of my skin?

I was 23 when I started frequenting my local
public bathhouse. The first few times being
completely naked around so many people,
who were busy scrubbing and cleaning, or not
at all busy but just sitting and soaking, were
intimidating. My boobs are bigger than the
average Japanese woman's, I'm curvy and I'm six
feet tall. They had a lot to stare at.

In the beginning, it was mostly me who did
the looking. All of the shapes, all of the different
kinds of bodies. And boobs. The boobs holding
on for dear life to the beautiful 98-year-old lady
from down the road, whose bended form I saw
in her vegetable patch every morning; the more
shapely 45-year-old bodies; the 60-something
lady from the supermarket; the young teenage
budding bodies; and the lovely, fresh toddlers
bursting with life. The chubby, the skinny, the
birth marked. Nobody lay down, posing in the
ridiculous ways we see on buildings – young
backs arched, shiny, pouting, pursed lips. We
were just a bunch of women enjoying our
evening ritual and relaxing before bed. Coming
and going. In and out of that bathhouse.

How beautiful, natural and normal ageing
bodies are when you see so many in such an
ordinary scene – no self-consciousness, it is all
a matter of course. A bath is a family pleasure,
a functional experience. I wish we had this
culture. It's nothing like the beach nudity we
have in Australia. Trust the Japanese to blend
function and routine with community and
cleanliness. So efficient!

WE BUY SAKE LEES IN A SHEET

SAKE LEES AS A KIND OF CHEESE REPLACEMENT

Whatever is going into a lot of the cheese replacements, soy 'sausages' and 'tastes like cheese, looks like meat' products isn't something I want to feed my family. Japanese people are also returning to their food roots – and how lucky for them, because they hadn't really left it for that long. Palates change, but they can be retrained. Cue: sake lees as a replacement for cheese. It's healthy, and a by-product.

Crackers

Yuko, who works at The Fermentary, got this inspiration from Teradahonke - wild kōji grower and sake maker just outside of Tokyo. These really do taste like they have cheese in them. Yeasty, delicious, dairy-free crackers. Umami GALORE.

20 g (¾ oz) sake lees, plus enough water to
    make it into a paste (see notes)
100 g (3½ oz) flour (any type)
2 tablespoons olive oil, plus extra for painting
1 teaspoon fine salt

EXTRA FLAVOURS (OPTIONAL)
1 teaspoon black sesame paste (sprinkle with
    black sesame seeds at the end)
1 teaspoon tahini (sprinkle with sesame seeds
    at the end)
1 teaspoon honey (sprinkle with herbs of your
    choice at the end)

Preheat the oven to 180°C (350°F).
    In a large bowl, massage the sake lees and water into a paste – this can take some work. Mix in the flour, olive oil, salt and any extra flavours you like, to form a dough. Roll out thinly, paint on some more olive oil and sprinkle on any seeds or herbs, if using. Cut to the shape you like and transfer to an oiled tray.

Bake for about 10 minutes, then turn the crackers over. Reduce the oven temperature to 160°C (320°F) and bake for a further 10 minutes, but keep an eye on them – they cook quickly.

Notes: *Instead of water you could use a brine from one of your vegetable ferments – like kimchi juice, for example. This will give you lovely flavour and colour. If you use kimchi juice it's nice to paint the crackers with sesame oil and sprinkle with Korean chilli flakes.*

I like to bake this as a whole sheet and then break it up to eat, but you can also make them into long sticks.

ROLLING OUT SAKE LEES CRACKER DOUGH

Condiments & dressings

(& other little adventures)

Fermenting and preservation in general brings out the survivalist in me – not the doomsday kind, rather the dreamy, off-the-grid-in-a-cabin-on-a-lake kind. I could arrive with a stash of dry goods such as wheat berries, quinoa, juniper berries, assorted nuts and dried herbs, some flours, salt, legumes and rice. And as long as I had water, a hot plate or oven, I could have a benchful of interesting ferments within a couple of days. There could be bubbling refreshing drinks, a jar of crackers, and some fluffy idli or dhosa the next day. Who needs a fridge? Get your hands on some milk and cream and with your kefir grains, you've got butter, yoghurt, cream cheeses and whey.

Here are a few lovely things that have, at different times, been my obsession ... part of my ferment *zanmai*. There are some dressings I have spoken about in this book, a few vinegar-based recipes and good mustard. And there are a couple of favourite things that didn't belong elsewhere, misfits that hang together, which might be your favourites. And most of these things are foods that don't need a fridge and could happily sit in the cupboard in your off-the-grid, slow-living life.

Fermented honey & garlic

Simple ferments that can stay on the shelf to pull from whenever I'd like are my favourite kind, and honey ferments are exactly that. Every workshop we do always ends with me talking about the magic of honey, even though we never plan it that way. People are drawn to the gorgeous jars of honey and bottles of mead on the shelves and never fail to ask about them.

It's important to use raw honey. Look for this on the label or buy from a local beekeeper.

You can add nigella seeds (*Nigella sativa*) to the garlic and honey, then look into adding these seeds to other ferments as well, both for their flavour and because they are historically very healing. A gentleman approached me at my stand at a market recently and told me that nigella seeds were said, by the Prophet Muhammad, to be 'good for all diseases except death', and that putting them with garlic and honey was even better. Score! Use of these little seeds is also documented as far back as the time of Cleopatra.

Take garlic-fermented honey as a syrup with some nigella like a medicine, or add it to a hot drink. Use the garlic in your cooking or eat one raw to fight colds. Great for sore throats!

The garlic can be replaced with jalapeño chillies, small red shallots and a small sprig of rosemary or oregano.

Raw honey is precious and can be rather expensive, but small items like garlic don't require too much. This recipe is so easy but you'll treasure it.

Preparation time: 10 minutes
Fermentation time: 7+ days
Equipment: 750+ ml (25½+ fl oz) jar with a lid or air-lock system, weight

garlic, enough to fill the jar three-quarters full
1 tablespoon nigella seeds (optional)
raw honey, enough to cover the garlic

Fill the jar three-quarters full with peeled garlic and, if using, sprinkle in the nigella seeds.

Pour the honey over the garlic carefully, waiting for it to settle before pouring some more. Move the garlic around with a chopstick, making sure the honey fills every hole.

Weigh the garlic down with something like a glass disc, as it's better to keep the garlic under the honey.

Lid with an air-lock system (or use a normal seal, place the jar on a plate and be sure to check on it every 24 hours to release the gas).

Check it the next day as the garlic tends to rise, so you'll need to push it back down under the honey again. As the honey becomes more liquid it will be easier to push the garlic down.

Keep checking on your jar as the ferment can get quite fizzy. If you aren't using an air-lock, you should release some gas from time to time until it stops.

Leave for a week or so. The honey takes on an amazing flavour and can be used straight away if you wish – any way you'd like.

FERMENTED
HONEY & GARLIC

Note: *The garlic cloves may take a while longer before they impress you with their development. However, this honeyed and fermented garlic is divine. Pull a clove out as needed to slice finely or chop and add to anything you can imagine a honeyed garlic clove belongs. I keep ours on the shelf to keep aging, but if you are afraid of botulism then keep it in the fridge. (Or don't make it.)*

FERMENTED HONEY & GARLIC LOVES:

— lamb chops – chop a clove and sprinkle on your lamb chop, and add a little of the honey before barbecuing or grilling

— blue cheese – pour the garlic-infused honey over a thin slice of baguette

— labneh – use as oil to store it

— yoghurt (particularly smoked yoghurt) – drizzle it over a bowlful

— stir-fries, dressings and marinades – finely

chop a garlic clove and add or use the honey

— cheese platters

— being used as a replacement for regular garlic – put it under the skin of a chicken in a roast

— healing – take a tablespoon for a sore throat or to ward off a cold

— Fire tonic (page 158) or cider – add some to either.

Mustard

I didn't know how easily mustards could be made until quite recently. In fact, I don't think I'd ever even thought about mustard other than buying and eating it. I've enjoyed some special flavoured mustards, and paid a lot extra for them (I am guilty of being easily seduced by packaging).

As with many of the recipes in this book, there are very few ingredients – mustard seeds, a liquid and an acid. You can play around with other additions such as herbs and spices or how sweet or hot you'd like it, but the basic recipe and technique is the same.

And if you want to delve further and look for the science, it's there. The heat that you may seek is released from within the seeds but will be greatly reduced if you warm it up. So when you add your liquid you can keep it cold to make sure the seeds remain potent, or warm the liquid to make it milder. We like to keep the liquid room temperature, particularly because we often use kimchi or kraut juice as the liquid. I also frequently add some of our garlic or jalapeño fermented honey as a sweetener (see page 200). When I ferment honey and garlic with mustard in mind, I also ferment some sage into the honey and get a beautiful subtle honey–sage mustard.

Preparation time: 15 minutes
Fermentation time: 2 days–2 months
Equipment: 2 small jars

1 cup brown mustard seeds
1 cup yellow mustard seeds
1 tablespoon salt (less if you've substituted with a salty liquid)
250 ml (8½ fl oz/1 cup) liquid (water, wine, beer, kimchi juice, etc)
125 ml (4 fl oz/½ cup) acidic liquid such as apple cider vinegar
extra flavourings, as you desire (for example, honey, sage, black garlic)

Mix the mustard seeds and grind about half of them into a powder in a food processor or using a mortar and pestle (tough gig). Combine the powdered and whole seeds, add the salt and liquid and let the mixture steep for about 10 minutes before adding your acidic liquid.

Jar it up and seal with a regular lid, then put it in the fridge for at least 2 days, but aim for a month. I choose a month, but you could open it up to show off, or take a swipe for a sandwich, chunk of cheese or dressing …

Take it out of the fridge after a month, add your flavours (if using) and put it on the bench for another month. We generally start eating it before a month – but the older it gets, the deeper the flavours. When the month is up, you can put it in the fridge, give to friends, spread over your corned beef … whatever you like. It will keep for a very long time.

Kimchi–tahini spread

Mix either kimchi paste, a bit of juice from your jar or finely chopped kimchi through some tahini (or a good nut butter). Alternatively, when you get near the end of your kimchi jar, add

MIXED MUSTARD
SEEDS

some tahini (or nut butter) and mix it through
and eat as is.

You could make it finer by blending it and
then spreading on bread or crackers, or to use
under avocado on toast, for example.

OR add a bit of coconut cream, adjusting the
flavours as you go to get the perfect sauce for
chicken skewers or any tofu dish. You could also
add some to the centre of a rice ball (*onigiri*) or
plonk some onto warm rice. No kidding, this
is delicious. Black sesame paste is good too,

although the colour won't be as lovely as the
tahini version.

Wasabi mayonnaise

I often just grab some Japanese kewpie
mayonnaise (even though I know it's bad for you)
and add a pinch of wasabi powder. Alternatively,
make your own mayonnaise or substitute
mayonnaise for an avocado instead.

Be careful when buying wasabi in a tube –
be sure you're getting real wasabi and not just
horseradish with green colouring. Good wasabi
is expensive, but you only need a little. We've
got a plant now – the leaves are lovely, but we
haven't pulled the wasabi yet. Fingers crossed.

Kimchi mayonnaise

I mentioned earlier that when you make your
kimchi, it's handy to keep aside some of the
paste to use. Add a teaspoon to some crème
fraîche or mayonnaise – this is great for dipping
fried food like hot chips, little meatballs or
chicken, for example.

A touch in some tamari or soy sauce with
gyoza goes beautifully as well.

Indian lime pickle

I love lime pickle. Its acidity goes really well
with an oily curry or any rich, heavy dish. It's an
accompaniment – not something to eat on its
own necessarily.

It's called a pickle but really it's a ferment and
good for your gut. There is a touch of vinegar –
this helps to soften the limes. This is a great
tinkering task for me as I love to check on it
and push the limes under the juices as they
increase; the heady aroma coming from it as you
do that is divine. Also you get a month to go and
buy some asafoetida. There's a second ferment
period similar to the mustard – you need to pull
the limes out and add oil and spices.

Preparation: 15 minutes
Fermentation time: 5–6 weeks
Equipment: 2 L (68 fl oz) wide-mouthed jar, jar
for storing

FIRST FERMENT
20 limes, cut into eighths or smaller
4 tablespoons salt
3 tablespoons ground turmeric
1 tablespoon white vinegar

A MONTH LATER
250 ml (8½ fl oz/1 cup) oil, such as sunflower
    or olive oil
1 teaspoon asafoetida
½ cup mustard seeds
¼ cup fenugreek seeds, crushed (they are hard
    to crush by hand – use a grinder)
1 tablespoon cayenne pepper

In a small bowl, toss the limes with the salt,
turmeric and vinegar.

Transfer to the jar, cover and let it ferment
for 4 weeks, stirring or stamping down at least
daily. I just place a lid loosely on top because
I like the easy access to stamp the limes down
whenever I go by. The limes will slowly give in
and tenderise.

After 4 weeks (I hope you have the asafoetida
by now!) add the oil, asafoetida, mustard seeds,
fenugreek and cayenne pepper. Mix well.

Ferment for another 1–2 weeks, still pushing
down on the limes if you like. At this stage judge
whether you'd like to keep the lime pieces the
same size, or pop them into a processor for
more of a chutney texture.

Jar it up into a sterilised jar, lid and place in
the fridge. It probably keeps for years, but it only
ever lasts a month or two here. We like it with
plain rice or with a curry.

Carrots pickled in oil

Preparation time: 15 minutes
Fermentation time: 1 week
Equipment: 1 L (34 fl oz) jar with tight lid (no air-lock system)

1 teaspoon salt
2 teaspoons black mustard seeds
1 teaspoon nigella seeds
1 teaspoon black pepper
1 teaspoon cayenne pepper
500 g (1 lb 2 oz) carrots, peeled and chopped into angular bite-sized pieces
500 ml (17 fl oz/2 cups) sunflower oil

Crush the salt, seeds, black pepper and cayenne pepper together using a mortar and pestle or powerful grinder.

Pop the carrots into the jar, followed by the spice mix. Warm the oil and then pour to cover the carrots. Tightly lid your jar and shake well to mix the spice mixture around. Leave in a warm spot for a week, shaking at least once daily.

Don't serve the oil, just shake the jar first and pull out a few carrots. Serve the pieces of carrot as you would a relish. Keep in the fridge or cupboard for a few months.

Ginger pickle (gari) for your sushi pleasure

Traditionally, pickled ginger is used as a palate cleanser between sushi courses, but now it has usually become just part of sushi presentation and is made pink with artificial colours. Only very young ginger will give you a natural pink tinge, so with the regular ginger available in the shops you may want to add a colour via some beet juice or red shiso leaves, as shown in the recipe method.

Preparation time: 20 minutes + 30 minutes steeping
Equipment: 500 ml (17 fl oz) jar

about 300 g (10½ oz) fresh ginger
1 teaspoon salt
2 tablespoons sugar
about 125 ml (4 fl oz/½ cup) rice vinegar
2 red shiso leaves, or a dash of beetroot (beet) juice (optional)

Peel and slice the ginger – a mandoline does this beautifully. (If you are lucky and have young ginger, peeling is unnecessary, plus I like it a bit rustic.) Sprinkle with the salt and 1 tablespoon of the sugar and let sit for about half an hour. Don't rinse.

In a saucepan of boiling water, blanch the ginger for just 1 minute (and only 20 seconds if using young ginger).

Drain off the water and transfer the ginger to a sterilised jar.

In a saucepan over high heat, combine the vinegar and the remaining tablespoon of sugar, and add the shiso leaves or beet juice if you'd like a pink hue. Boil until the sugar has dissolved (and the colour emerges from the shiso). Remove the shiso leaves and then pour the liquid over the ginger, before lidding. It should be ready within 3 days and will keep in the fridge for at least 3 months.

Note: *Don't limit yourself to using this purely as a sushi condiment – there are many ways a sweet pickled ginger can be used. It's delicious in salads, particularly a soba noodle salad.*

Garlic or shallots in soy

Preparation time: 10 minutes
Fermentation time: 1+ weeks
Equipment: 1 L (34 fl oz) jar, weight (optional)

about 50 garlic cloves, unpeeled, or 10 shallots
    peeled (or enough to fill your jar)
500 ml (17 fl oz/2 cups) rice vinegar
enough water to cover the garlic/shallots
500 ml (17 fl oz/2 cups) soy sauce
2 tablespoons sake
4 tablespoons sugar

Place the garlic or shallots in the jar. Add
the vinegar and enough water to cover them
completely – if necessary, use a weight to keep
them under the liquid. Seal the jar. After 1–2
weeks, strain off the liquid and transfer them to
a clean jar.

In a small saucepan over high heat, boil the
soy sauce, sake and sugar until the sugar has
dissolved, let cool, then pour this mixture over
the garlic or shallots. This will sit on the bench
or in the fridge for at least 6 months.

Note: *You don't need to peel the garlic for this;
they are lovely just cut at the tips and squeezed
into your mouth. If it's young garlic you'll be
able to eat them skin and all*

Fermented hot sauce

Preparation time: 15 minutes
Fermentation time: 2 weeks–3 months
Equipment: 1 L (34 fl oz) jar with air-lock system,
follower, weight, bottle for storing

9 large red chillies (or enough to fill your jar –
    see notes)
2–5 garlic cloves, peeled

1 red onion, sliced
1 litre (34 fl oz/4 cups) water
2 tablespoons fine salt
pinch of sugar

Take the stems off the chillies, trying to keep
them whole. Pack the garlic, onion and chillies
tightly into the jar.

Make a brine by mixing the water and salt
in a jug and stirring until dissolved. Pour the
brine over, making sure to cover the chillies, but
leaving headroom.

Weigh the chillies down with a follower and
weights in the same way you would for a brine
ferment (page 68). Seal the jar with an air-lock.

Ferment for between 2 weeks and 3 months.

Strain, reserving the liquid. Blitz the chillies
in a food processor, adding the liquid as you go
to get the consistency you'd like.

Pour into a sterilised bottle and store in the
fridge. It will last in the fridge for 6–12 months.
(No, it won't. You'll eat it all or give it away
before then.)

Notes: *For fermenting, it's best to buy local
(not imported) chillies, as you need to avoid
the possibility of them having been sprayed
and the wild yeasts destroyed. There are a lot
of varieties out there. The hotter the chilli, the
hotter the sauce, obviously. I usually just buy
what is available, and always use a variety.*

*If you'd like to make the sauce shelf-stable,
you'll need to add some vinegar and heat it up,
preserve-style. To do this, when blitzing the
ingredients together after fermentation, add
60 ml (2 fl oz/¼ cup) of white vinegar per 1 litre
(34 fl oz/4 cups) of sauce. You'll also need to
heat the sealed containers of chilli sauce in a
water bath: boil your jars or bottles in a large
pan of boiling water. Fill with the sauce while
the bottles are still hot. Lid and place in a large
pot of boiling water over high heat, deep enough*

that the water doesn't cover them, but so the water reaches almost as far as the lids. Boil like this for 10 minutes. Take them out, allow to cool, and label.

This won't be a raw ferment anymore, but the flavour will still be there, and I don't consider hot sauce a source of probiotics, so I often preserve it.

Idli & dhosa

I hadn't connected that dhosa and idli were ferments until I made them at Sandor Katz's. Up until then, I associated them with food vans, share plates and Indian restaurants. Varma, our partner at The Fermentary, brought me an idli pan after a trip home and soon idli became our newest love.

First, you ferment the batter for idli and save the rest, leaving it out on the bench or in the fridge for the dhosa batter. Both are popular with the kids; small versions of them star in their lunchboxes with all sorts of condiments.

You really need a powerful blender to get the wet grains to a consistency that works well. Idli require their own special pan, but dhosa do not. The best idli seems to come from using 'cream of rice' – which is really just ground rice and reminds me of my childhood for some reason. Maybe it was baby food? When Varma brought cream of rice over I didn't want to use it because I was trying to be a purist, but he insisted that's what his aunty uses so that was that. And the idli was much fluffier actually.

Idli

You may have to add this to your list of another pan to buy ... an idli pan has little cups that you place the dough in and then you sit it into a pot of steaming water. It's steamed bread.

Preparation time: 12 hours–overnight
Fermentation time: 24 hours
Equipment: jars, idli pan

200 g (7 oz/1 cup) rice, ground (or buy 'cream of rice')
250 g (9 oz/1 cup) lentils
ghee or coconut oil, for greasing

Place the rice and lentils in separate jars and cover generously with water. Cover with a cloth and leave on your kitchen bench, or in a warm place, to sit for 12 hours or overnight. After soaking, strain and reserve some of the water in another bowl in case you need to add some liquid later.

Blitz the rice and lentils separately in a food processor, adding a bit of the reserved liquid if you need it – you are after a smoothie/pancake batter consistency.

Mix the blended rice and lentils together now – the colour is gorgeous.

Transfer the mixture to a bowl or another jar to ferment for about 24 hours. We put ours on the bench above our dishwasher, which is lovely and warm. It should rise slightly, even doubling in quantity by morning. (Mark the level with some tape so you can monitor its progress if you like that kind of thing.)

The next day, grease your idli pans with some ghee or coconut oil and spoon some of the mixture into each cup. Sit the idli cups in a saucepan of simmering water over low heat, close the lid and let them steam. They take about 10 minutes and are ready when they are light and fluffy. If they come out rubbery, then you've botched it up. Sorry. We eat those anyway, sorry and confused.

Ferment your batter further in the fridge for more idli tomorrow, or just use to make dhosa later (see the next recipe).

Dhosa

Dhosa are like crêpes only better in my opinion because they are slightly chewy ... or at least they are when I make them. We might make them a bit too thick and slightly overdone, but we like them this way, maybe because it reminds the girls of grilled mochi. They are great with a curry or to actually house a curry – all wrapped up like a burrito – or just to rip and dip.

Make the dough as for idli, leaving it a day longer if you like. Grease a crêpe-style frying pan and pour the batter in as you would for a crêpe. Flip and keep warm while you do the rest. I'm pretty bad at spreading crêpes, dhosas and injera, but my kids don't mind a bit. Still tastes good.

Injera

This lovely sour crêpe-like bread serves as your plate and utensils. Different to crêpes, injera is only cooked on one side – the large bubbles that form on top are perfect for catching sauces. Pop the injera over your plate, plop your curry on top and tear bits of bread off to carry the curry up and into your mouth. They use huge round pans to make these as big as platters in restaurants. I want one!

Injera is traditionally made with teff flour and water alone. The short fermentation will give it a bit of an airy, chewy feel and a lovely sour taste. We used only teff and water when we made injera at Sandor's, but when nothing was happening on the second day, we added a touch of sourdough leaven to help it along.

I've always ended up adding a bit of starter; perhaps our teff has been treated quite a bit before packaging. Start off as you would a sourdough mother – by just sitting the mixed batter of teff flour and water to ferment for 1–3 days. If you notice that nothing is really happening or if you'd like to ensure a good ferment, give it a little help by adding a dash of any of your living brews or a dollop of sourdough mother/leaven. Milk kefir is my favourite 'helper' and always makes a great starter for any flours, particularly for the pancake kind.

Preparation time: 5 minutes
Fermentation time: overnight–3 days
Makes: about 5 injera (depending on size)

210 g (7½ oz/1½ cups) teff flour
500 ml (17 fl oz/2 cups) lukewarm water
drop of starter, such as milk kefir or baking powder (optional)
pinch of salt

Combine your teff flour and water, then mix in your chosen starter. Cover with a breathable cloth and let sit overnight or for a few days. The dough will rise or even appear a little hard on the surface, but become more liquid again upon stirring.

Grease a crêpe pan and place over medium heat. Pour in the batter in circles, starting from the outside and going into the middle, and cover with a lid. (You may need to fashion a lid yourself for your pan if it doesn't have one. You only cook injera on one side, so the top needs the heat gained from a lid. Little hint: use aluminium foil.)

The first injera will take a couple of minutes, but after that they should cook quite quickly. Bubbles should form on the top – larger than on a normal pancake. See if you can slide the injera off your pan and onto a waiting plate without ripping it. If you have something quite thin to slide it onto that would be great – in Ethiopia they have woven platters for that.

My *zanmai* to yours

I wish you many periods of *zanmai* in your life. And may one of them be a 'ferment zanmai'. *Zanmai* is a Japanese term derived from Sanskrit meaning 'to be luxuriously absorbed in something of great interest'. My wish is for you to find all the time for this 'ferment zanmai' you need.

I am only here now because of all the different places and times in my life where I was curious and somehow got caught up in a ferment of some kind. Not that I called it *zanmai* then; not once did I stop to think that each *zanmai* was actually connected to my last – it just felt like a natural progression. Other times, I went into a *zanmai* that was completely different, like learning to knit or sew, during which I gave family and friends my works made with beautiful and expensive wool, but little skill. I loved it though. It's often not until you are in the middle of something that you realise you are in it, right?

Roger and I love the cacophony of sounds from our kids, their music and their friends in our home. We also get simple pride from the sounds coming from our pantry (fermenting) bench. Those sounds symbolise life, a successful batch.

My business came about because of a need to fix my youngest daughter's gut. I was struck, dumbfounded really, when I drew a direct line between all of my hobbies and found that most of them involved fermentation and therefore probiotic-rich food of some kind. I went forward equipped and steadfast that this was easy and she would be okay. I had a job and a purpose as well, which as anyone with an unwell loved one would know, is very important.

My mission was never completed though because now I am on a journey to get everyone else I know and meet to go back to our very roots and somehow start a journey of simplifying and making from scratch, and to at least choose one ferment that somehow holds their heart, takes their breath away. Take a stand on over-consumption and industry-led consumerism. Connect with others and share what you know. Or just choose another *zanmai*, that's good too.

Thanks!

To our loyal clientele – retailers, distributors and customers everywhere – thanks for loving our work. Also of course to our early customers, adopters and believers, and critics of The Ferm. To the vegans who loved us enough to ask us for a vegan kimchi. To all believers in real slow food.

To anyone who has ever worked at The Fermentary. To Varma Prasada, our appreciation and respect for your hard work and dedication runs deep. Gratitude to the now quite long termer and fellow dreamer, Yuko Dhani-Legg.

To a couple of very special friends – buoys for me – your spiritual advice, ear, massive wine-drinking ability and loving support are cherished. To Cheryl Norman and Robyn Patton. To Lynn Connors Smith and her family for always sending us what we need, whether it's encouragement, love, belief, trust – or a tent and sleeping bag. To my own parents who made a nomadic army upbringing feel rich and lucky, which made my life seem full of possibility. And for supporting me no matter which trajectory I was selling them.

To my handful of first early partners in The Ferm – the mixed crew who made me feel like the business was a good idea and could be something. To Katherine Ivanac for my first grains and start of a business, Gabe McAuley and Stephanie Duboudin. And then Wendy Fowler and Michael Dhillon and Bindi for the early support, late-night work, reno of the shed, storage space in your winery and your ear during a bit of a sad time for us all.

To photographers Victor Pugatshew, who is responsible for many of our best food pics, and Chris Le Messurier and James Broadway for the people ones. And naturally, to the magnificent Tara Pearce for the photos in this book and making me feel more 'breezy Sunday morning' than I ever felt possible. To Emma Jimson, who makes me the most divine crocks and ceramics.

To fermie friends everywhere for making the magic more visible and tangible. To Sandor Katz for introducing and inspiring me, and Miin Chan for the late-night chats. To Nancy Singleton Hachisu. Mark Turner – for your adventures in fermentation from afar. To the ladies at the writers' lunch with Annie Smithers who couldn't have realised what being at a table with strong, inspiring older women who still dream BIG meant to me. Kate Hill, Karen Rush, thank you.

To my food heroes, mentors, believers and good customers: Alla Wolf-Tasker, Maggie Beer, Stephanie Alexander, Guy Grossi, Matt Wilkinson, Dan Hunter, Alice Zavlavsky, Emma Dean, Christine Manfield and Roger Fowler.

To John Flynn – 'wasband' – long my best friend, dedicated dreamer, father to our girls, and travel partner for 20 years – dreaming and planning still. Your support, trust and ear have been vital and I'm proud of us. Your crazy happy spirit will outlive us all, which is both annoying and reassuring.

To Hardie Grant and Jane Willson for believing we could, Rachel Day for sorting my recipe style and wordy mess, Anna Collett for final touches, Jodi Wuestewald for her styling. Big love to Astred Cherry and Mark Campbell for helping to make this look so pretty.

To my daughters Bella, Lily and Lucia – for a love this deep and for being mine and each other's biggest fans, coaches, inspiration and critics. Such a bittersweet honour to witness your dreams and watch you grow. To Ryder and Willow for the last two years and to the future of our noisy, happy, busy home. All five taste-testing kids: thanks for your massages, hair-dos, cuddles, laughter, approval, encouragement, patience and love (and your praise of my bentos).

And to Roger Fowler – at first my partner in business and then in life. You made Melbourne our home, and filled in all the gaps while I got on with this. Thanks for your patience and help, for testing my recipes and reining me in a bit. I'm ever grateful for your unconditional support and for young love when we least expected it. x

Recommended reading

BEFORE YOUR RECOMMENDED READING ...
HERE'S A FINAL BIT ON GUT HEALTH

When you rinse with a mouthwash, or clean your hands with antibacterial sanitiser, you are killing the good bacteria and the bad and the in-between. You are killing it all. Your body isn't designed to have no life. It relies on it.

If you've been on the internet or watching TV or reading anything in the last few years, you'll have seen all the news on the research into gut health and its importance for our immune system, and into the very intimate connection between the gut microbiome and our brain.

We need the bad and the good bacteria in our bodies to thrive – the bad only become bad when there aren't any good to keep them honest. And calling them good and bad is a bit ... well, black and white. It's not as simple as that, which is why you are after a broad spectrum of bacteria in your living foods. And if those living foods also contain 'pre-biotics' – food for the bacteria to thrive once in your gut – then all the better. I don't focus on pre-biotics very much when I talk gut health because if you are eating real, whole foods most of the time you are bound to get these.

Don't 'take' your ferments like medicine. Aim to make them so delicious that you can easily incorporate them into your everyday. I encourage you to read up on gut health if you have an inkling that you may need to work on it for other reasons. Now, onto the recommended reading ...

GUT HEALTH

Natasha Campbell-McBride, *Gut and Psychology Syndrome: Natural Treatment for Autism, ADD/ADHD, Dyslexia, Dyspraxia, Depression, Schizophrenia*, Medinform Publishing, 2010.

Giulia Enders, *GUT: The Inside Story of Our Body's Most Under-rated Organ*, Scribe Publications, 2015.

Rob Knight, *Follow Your Gut: The Enormous Impact of Tiny Microbes*, Simon & Schuster, 2015.

BACTERIA

Theodore Rosebury, *Life on Man*, Viking Press, 1969. (This one is a bit old but I found it fascinating; it was written at the beginning of the household war on bacteria.)

Masayuki Ishikawa, *Moyasimon: Tales of Agriculture* series, Del Rey Books (Random House), 2005. (This is a lighter read – in fact it's Japanese anime about a boy who can see bacteria and SO fun.)

FERMENTATION

William Shurtleff, Akiko Aoyagi, *The Book of Miso*, 10 Speed Press, 1979.

Stephen Buhner, *Sacred and Healing Herbal Beers: The Secrets of Ancient Fermentation*, Siris Books, 1998.

Sandor Katz, *Wild Fermentation: The Flavor, Nutrition, and Craft of Live-Culture Foods*, Chelsea Green Publishing Co, 2003.

Ikuo Hisamatsu, *Quick and Easy Tsukemono: Japanese Pickling Recipes*, Japan Publications Trading Company, 2005.

Edward Farnworth (ed.), *Handbook of Fermented Functional Foods*, second edition, CRC Press, 2008.

Sandor Katz, *The Art of Fermentation*: *An In-depth Exploration of Essential Concepts and Processes from Around the World*, Chelsea Green Publishing Co, 2012.

Chad Robertson, *Tartine No. 3: Modern Ancient Classic Whole*, Chronicle Books, 2013.

David Asher, *The Art of Natural Cheesemaking*, Chelsea Green Press, 2015.

Nancy Singleton Hachisu, *Preserving the Japanese Way: Traditions of Salting, Fermenting, and Pickling for the Modern Kitchen*, Andrews McMeel Publishing, 2015.

GENERAL FOOD & DRINK

Mark Kurlansky, *Salt: A World History*, Penguin Books, 2002.

Tadashi Agi, Shu Okimoto, *Drops of God* series, Vertical Ink, 2004 onwards. (This continues the topic of 'gourmet manga'. I enjoy the sommelier story – all wines mentioned in the series are real, and the authors were ranked as powerful influencers of wine in Japan at the time.)

Tetsu Kariya and Akira Hanasaki, *Oishinbo: A la carte* series, Viz Media, Subs. of Shogakukan Inc, 2009 onwards. (This is one of my favourite food series in manga; the one on sake is great and on topic, but I do love them all.)

WEBSITES

All the SCOBYs, sake lees, kōji and other lovely fermentation accoutrements mentioned in the book are available for purchase online from our website: www.thefermentary.com.au. But there are also many different culture-share Facebook pages where you can buy and swap cultures, as well as lots of groups and festivals all over the world that celebrate specific ferments and fermentation in general. So keep your eyes out or get googling. Since I started this adventure these festivals have grown amazingly. If there isn't one near you – make your own group or festival. Do it!

Sandor Katz's website (www.wildfermentation.com) is also a great place to start. His Facebook page is also helpful. The website is full of FAQs, and if you can't find the right 'Q' then you can ask someone on the forum.

GET IN TOUCH

You can find and contact us online via our website or social media. Stay informed, share and get involved in the world of fermenting.

www: thefermentary.com.au

Facebook: TheFermentary

Instagram: @thefermentary

Twitter: @fermentary

Index

Published in 2017 by Hardie Grant Books, an imprint of Hardie Grant Publishing

Hardie Grant Books (Melbourne)
Building 1, 658 Church Street
Richmond, Victoria 3121

Hardie Grant Books (London)
5th & 6th Floors
52–54 Southwark Street
London SE1 1UN

hardiegrant.com/au/book

A catalogue record for this
book is available from the
National Library of Australia

NATIONAL
LIBRARY
OF AUSTRALIA

Ferment for good
ISBN 978 1 74379 209 4

Publishing Director: Jane Willson
Managing Editor: Marg Bowman
Project Editors: Rachel Day, Anna Collett
Editor: Rachel Day
Proofreader: Katri Hilden
Design Manager: Mark Campbell
Designer: Astred Hicks, Design Cherry
Illustrator: Astred Hicks, Design Cherry
Photographer: Tara Pearce
Stylist: Jodi Wuestewald
Production Manager: Todd Rechner
Production Coordinator: Rebecca Bryson

Thanks to Pom-me-granite and Bonnie & Neil for use of their props.
Special thanks to Natasha Morgan (natashamorgan.com.au) for welcoming the photo shoot to
her property, Oak and Monkey Puzzle, at Spargo Creek, Victoria.

Colour reproduction by Splitting Image Colour Studio
Printed in China by Leo Paper Product. LTD